LIGHT AND ATMOSPHERE IN WATERCOLOUR

T. Chamberlain 1993.

ATELIER SERIES

TREVOR CHAMBERLAIN

a personal view

LIGHT AND ATMOSPHERE IN WATERCOLOUR

TREVOR CHAMBERLAIN
WITH ANGELA GAIR

David & Charles

ACKNOWLEDGEMENTS

I would like to thank Angela Gair for her clear-minded enthusiasm in keeping me on track, and for producing such a cohesive, readable and inspiring text from my notes and ramblings. Without her this book would not have happened. My sincere thanks also to my old friend David Curtis for writing the foreword to the book, and to Clifford Borlase for his fine photography.

A DAVID & CHARLES BOOK
First published 1999

A catalogue record for this book is available from the British Library.

ISBN 0 7153 0845 9

Book design by Les Dominey Design Company, Exeter
Printed in Singapore by C. S. Graphics Pte Ltd. for David & Charles
Brunel House Newton Abbot Devon

Page 1
TREE WITH SPANISH MOSS, SOUTH CAROLINA
Watercolour, 7x10in (18x25cm)

Page 2
CANVAS AWNINGS, ASWAN BAZAAR
Watercolour, 14x10in (35x25cm)

Page 5
GARDEN, NEWBY HALL
Watercolour, 7x10in (18x25cm)

CONTENTS

FOREWORD BY *DAVID CURTIS* 6

INTRODUCTION 8

Chapter One: EARLY YEARS AND INFLUENCES 12

Chapter Two: METHODS AND MATERIALS 22

Chapter Three: LANDSCAPES 38

Chapter Four: MARINE AND COASTAL 64

Chapter Five: TOWNSCAPES 84

Chapter Six: FIGURES 106

Chapter Seven: INDOOR SUBJECTS 120

INDEX 128

FOREWORD

Within each generation of painters there emerges an occasional special talent, able to observe a subject *en plein air* and capture its qualities to stunning effect. Such a master of this demanding 'on-site' approach to watercolour is Trevor Chamberlain.

Here, at last, is a comprehensive celebration of this painter's gift as a watercolourist. Within these pages you will gain an insight into his acute observation of subjects on a grand scale as well as some charming cameos of everyday life and events. Throughout his work, Trevor's passion for expressing the effects of light is evident, and he is always searching out that special 'feel' for the subject. On many occasions, I have witnessed Trevor's extraordinary eye for a subject and its compositional value, and his ability to capture the very best of any fleeting light effect or figurative content which may occur during the execution of the piece. His paintings are almost always finished on location – the true measure of the man and his craft.

The French Impressionist painter Camille Pissarro wrote in 1893, 'Blessed are they that see beautiful things in humble places where other people see nothing!' In this respect Trevor is indeed blessed, for he can find inspiration in the rusting hull of an old boat, a puddle in the road, or some forgotten corner of a field – subjects many of us would pass by without noticing. I deem him to be one of the finest painters of his genre – an opinion reflected in the immense following he has attained over the years.

Trevor has completed over fifty years of serious painting in the field. His diversity of subject matter, both at home and abroad, is truly a feast for the eye. It is an honour and a pleasure to have been asked to write this foreword for such a distinguished and celebrated artist.

DAVID CURTIS ROI, RSMA

LIGHT ON THE FORESHORE, DEPTFORD
Watercolour, 7x10in (18x25cm)

T. Chamberlain

INTRODUCTION

I was born and brought up on the edge of a Hertfordshire market town close to the countryside, so I have always identified with the great outdoors. In fact, when I was in my twenties I considered taking up mushroom farming or horticulture; this, I reasoned, would enable me to support myself while painting, without having to work in a stuffy office. I quickly realized, however, that this type of work involved long hours and would leave me with no time at all to pursue my artistic interests.

In all the years I have been painting my love of nature's moods and the effects of weather, atmosphere and light have never diminished. I am still completely enthralled by the myriad subtle effects experienced out of doors, and I'm always looking at things about me and seeing them in terms of paint. (Whilst driving through the countryside I have been known to mount the kerb when a lovely sunset or the light on a group of trees has caught my eye; and when I'm a passenger I find myself pressing my nose to the window, absorbing everything I pass: I can't bear to miss anything!)

The terror of the Second World War generated within me an indelible awareness of mortality and an appreciation that our time here is short – and this seems to have sharpened my awareness and appreciation of the things life has to offer. Consequently, in my

NAGHSHE-ROSTAM, NEAR SHIRAZ
Watercolour,
14x21½in (35x54cm)

WAPPING HIGH STREET, EVENING
Watercolour,
7x10in (18x25cm)

paintings I try to arrest time by capturing a beautiful moment to somehow make it live on. Some people do not seem to realize how precious is the period we are allotted on this earth and take things for granted. I tend to savour each day as if my last, appreciating and using fully (I hope) this God-given talent for painting I am lucky enough to have.

I am not a topographical painter, but seek to create an impression of nature and the spirit and atmosphere of a particular locality, rather than a precise representation. Painting outdoors, *sur le motif*, allows me to create an immediate record of my emotional response to nature, and I find the rapid and free-flowing qualities of watercolour ideally suited to capturing the fickle movement of light, which changes with each successive and evaporating moment. When I lay down washes on damp paper I am constantly surprised by what emerges, the fluid colours miraculously fusing and blending into semblances of clouds, fields, trees, figures and animals. I love the ease and weightlessness of watercolour and the way it allows me to incorporate chance effects. The outcome can sometimes be unpredictable, and some of the medium's most attractive effects are the result of accidents that can be induced but never entirely planned. I find such exhilaration in knowing that I am treading a narrow line between triumph and disaster.

The difficulty is that the painter must be in control in order to harness the qualities and characteristics of the medium. The caricatured image of Victorian maiden aunts painting flowers and picturesque views has encouraged the mistaken belief that watercolour is a gentle, undemanding art. Certainly watercolour painting requires less paraphernalia than oil painting, is less messy and definitely less smelly. And it does look deceptively easy: seductive washes of colour flowing and blending effortlessly on the paper can create superficially pleasing effects in a trice.

The truth is, of course, that watercolour is a subtle, complex and demanding medium and quite difficult to master; it is really rather cerebral if you're doing it properly. With an opaque medium like oils you can rework passages, changing your mind and correcting as you go along. Watercolour offers no such luxury, its transparency demanding that you work progressively from light to dark. A light colour cannot be applied over a dark one, and the characteristic luminosity of the medium is lost when too many washes are overlaid. This means that a lot of mental pre-planning is required before brush meets paper. You must always have a strategy, think several moves ahead and be aware of the consequences of every mark made.

An English art critic recently summed up the challenge of watercolour painting in a nutshell: 'To build up a composition in washes from light to dark, while leaving patches of white paper to represent the highlights, requires the forward planning of a chess player, the concentration of a Zen master, and the dexterity of a brain surgeon.' There are no shortcuts in watercolour painting and success can only come through dedication and sound observation from nature. Frequent practice alone will generate the necessary confidence when tackling the expressive, exciting, sometimes baffling medium of watercolour.

Opposite
FOG, SNOW AND ICE
Watercolour, 7x10in (18x25cm)

I enjoy painting winter landscapes; there's an added satisfaction when a painting comes off after enduring the freezing conditions. Whilst I was working in the snowy silence, a deer suddenly appeared out of the mist, froze briefly when it saw me and then was gone. Such are the magical moments we on-site painters encounter.

This was painted on Cotman paper, which has a sympathetic surface. The washes took a long time to dry in the damp air, but just before they dried I worked in some more positive shapes in the foreground. As the paper was still slightly damp, the edges of these shapes are quite soft: any sharp edges would have ruined the effect of morning haze. You have to gauge it just right, though. If the paper is too wet the colour fans out into the surrounding wash and you end up with an awful mess.

Above
GRAVEL QUARRY, BENGEO
Watercolour, 7x10in (18x25cm)

I live in an area rich in gravel deposits, so scenes such as this are very familiar to me. By no stretch of the imagination could this be termed a picturesque subject; nevertheless, I found the afternoon sunlight on the warm colour of the pit face, contrasting with the cool cast shadows across the undulating floor of the quarry most appealing. I was aware of the subtle changes in tone and colour of the sandy surfaces, and particularly liked the cool colour of the crane cabin set against the yellow machinery shed. This centre of interest is underlined by the strong 'V' shape formed by the shed roof and the long crane jib, which also cuts through the high horizon. The mechanical digger to the left counterbalances the main interest. I have tried to suggest the steel latticework of the jib by indicating a few light and dark struts.

Chapter One

EARLY YEARS AND INFLUENCES

Opposite
THE LEA AT WARE, 1996
Watercolour, 9¾x7in (24x18cm)

The Jesuits were right when they said 'give me the boy of seven and I will show you the man', because I have loved painting ever since I was that age, and even earlier. My father was a painter and decorator, and my first encounter with paints was at the tender age of five, when I conducted some illicit experiments with his household decorating paints. Predictably, the results were far from encouraging! I couldn't understand why the colours were running all over the place, and I wondered how people managed to produce pictures with them.

At school my best subject was art and when I was twelve my teacher encouraged me to join the local art class at the Ware Evening Institute, which was tutored by Alfred Wright (1900–97), a prominent local artist who was also a distant relative. Many students' first experience of art class consists of painting a dreary still life in some dingy classroom, but I was one of the lucky ones: on my very first evening, Wright took us out into the local countryside to paint the River Lea (I blushingly present the fruits of my labours below).

THE LEA AT WARE, 1946
Watercolour, 6x10in (15x25cm)

For sentimental reasons I have always kept that first attempt at watercolour painting. As you can see, I had a lot to learn at that stage about painting light! The viewer would never guess that it was painted on a sunny evening, because I made the classic beginner's mistake of concentrating on getting the local colours 'right' instead of recording how those colours are affected by the prevailing light. The version on page 13 was painted fifty years later (remarkably, the scene is still very much as it was back in 1946) and displayed alongside the first version in an exhibition of my work entitled *Light and Life; a Celebration of Fifty Years of Painting* at the Tryon and Swan Gallery in London. This time, I went for the drama of evening light and the dark sky throwing up the colours and tones of the scene. The other difference is that I used a portrait format because I wanted to make more of the reflections in the water.

That first experience of painting outdoors, directly from nature, was a revelation, and I have never stopped since. I owe Wright a great debt as it was he who taught me how to 'see', how to look for the subtle tones and colours in the landscape, the play of light and shadow and the pearly greys in the distance. Wright later introduced me to oil painting (he was an oil painter himself), and since I found oils easier to master than watercolour they gradually took over. I was greatly influenced by Van Gogh at the time, having seen an exhibition of his paintings at the Tate Gallery in London. The sheer vigour of his work and his use of thick impasto made an enormous impression on me, and many of my early oil paintings were painted quite thickly, often with a knife. Yet I also loved the early work of Victor Pasmore, which was very different from Van Gogh's. Before he turned to abstract painting, Pasmore used to paint very atmospheric, evocative landscapes and interiors. They were mostly oils, but they could almost have been watercolours, so delicate and wash-like was his use of paint.

At about that time Eadred Lutyens, nephew of the great Victorian architect Sir Edwin Lutyens, was running an informal weekly class in architectural drawing at his office, and I was invited to join. These classes helped to develop my imagination and drawing ability and stimulated an interest in architecture. My art training was otherwise informal, drawing on these early encouragements and influences, and I am mostly self-taught. Though my parents were willing to make sacrifices so that I could go to art school, I preferred to paddle my own canoe. I wasn't really interested in learning the theory of painting – I wanted to live it!

On leaving school in 1949 I worked for three years as a draughtsman cum general dogsbody in an ecclesiastical architect's office. During this time I led something of a double life: by day I earned my living making formal architectural drawings, but on evenings and weekends I was free to pursue my true vocation, which was to paint light and nature. In the early 1950s cars were a luxury few could afford and so I would venture out into the countryside on my bicycle. I strapped my easel to the crossbar and my painting box to the handlebars, and carried a board or canvas in one hand while steering with the other. It was all very precarious, and to do that today would be dicing with death, but I was full of youthful determination to get out there and paint, no matter what.

Though I didn't paint in watercolour myself at that stage, I certainly had a love and appreciation of the medium. My watercolour heroes were Jack Merriott (1901–68) and George Ayling (1887–1960). They were both traditional watercolourists and used the medium in a very fluid, wet way – something which I would have wished to achieve in my own watercolour paintings. Both were well-known painters in their day, but they are sadly overlooked and forgotten now. I remember first seeing Merriott's work when travelling to

A PEA-SOUPER ON THE THAMES, 1946
Watercolour, 6½ x 9½in (16x24cm)

This picture was actually painted in 1996. The Royal Society of Marine Artists celebrated its fiftieth anniversary that year, and members were invited to paint a marinescape portraying any occasion within that fifty-year timespan. The picture was painted mostly from imagination and memory, and recalls my thirteenth birthday, in 1946. I remember walking home from school that day through a real pea-souper of a fog. I got the idea of painting a picture of the Thames as I imagine it might have looked on that day: it would have been a very different scene from today, as London was then one of the busiest ports in the world. The scene is based on Rotherhithe, a part of the river I know well, and I have added the ships, barges, tugs and so on, as well as the warehouses and cranes looming out of the fog, from memory, my knowledge of the site, and my years of experience of painting ships.

London by train. Back then, in the glory days of steam engines, the railway companies commissioned some of the leading watercolour painters of the day, including Merriott, Rowland Hilder and Charles Knight, to depict scenes from all around Britain to be displayed as prints in the passenger compartments. These prints always had a long, narrow format and were usually panoramic landscapes. I would clamber into the carriage wondering which ones I was going to see, and I got to know them all.

Another great influence on my work was a local painter and teacher, Edward Archibald Brown, ARCA (1866–1935). He died when I was a baby, but he taught Alfred Wright, who in turn taught me at the Ware Evening Institute. Brown would cycle the lanes around his Hertford home, painting local scenes in oils in all seasons and all weathers. His paintings were very atmospheric, very 'English'. He found beauty in prosaic scenes such as a field of turnips, and would often comment on the sparkling colour of the sun after rain or the dull light before a storm. I empathized strongly with the sort of work that he did and of course was able to identify with the places he painted. Even now, when

Opposite
ST. PAUL'S AFTER THE BLITZ
(JACK MERRIOTT)
Watercolour, 13x16in (33x40cm)

In 1971 an exhibition was held in Arundel, Sussex, to celebrate the silver jubilee of the Wapping Group of Artists. This painting was on sale and I bought it because I had long wanted to own an example of Jack Merriott's work. Though I never met him, Merriott made a major contribution to my development as a watercolour painter. This picture was painted in 1943. As well as being a fascinating and moving historical document of a defining moment in the Second World War, it portrays the scene on an early, misty morning, a particular atmosphere which I am always fascinated by. Notice how simple is the handling of the rubble and debris, yet it tells the full story. The restrained palette lends the image a quiet dignity, and the tiny figures poking about in the debris add a particular poignancy and speak volumes about the scale, not only of the great cathedral but also of the disaster that is war.

Above
THE LANE TO BENGEO
(EDWARD ARCHIBALD BROWN)
Pencil, 5x7½in (12x19cm)

E. A. Brown was a local artist who influenced not just my painting but also my way of looking at nature and the landscape. I recognize many of the places he drew and painted, which haven't changed at all. Recently I was fortunate to have the opportunity of buying a batch of his drawings, of which this is an example. The drawings are exquisite, almost like paintings in themselves. The pencil work is very dense, yet incredibly fine and delicate. I marvel at Brown's ability to capture a particular atmosphere, purely with tone and no colour. On the back of each drawing he made copious notes about the time of day and the weather, rather as Constable did. The reverse of this one reads: 'The Lane to Bengeo, evening sun, 7.30. Aug 8, 1933. After a very hot day. (Brown, dried grass in the fore field. There were many bathers in next field)'.

I am out painting locally I often see the ghost of Brown; some of the places I paint have hardly changed at all since his day.

In 1953 came a sudden and unwelcome break in my painting career when I was called up for National Service. I did a two-year stint in the army and I don't mind admitting that I loathed it. It was the worst time of my life and I was so miserable that I did no painting at all. The only solace I found was in listening to music, but somehow I couldn't face painting. Still, I suppose I was lucky really, because my two years' service fell between the Korean War and the Suez crisis. The patron saint of artists must have been looking after me!

On leaving the army I worked for several years as an architectural draughtsman, and even though I enjoyed the work, I never lost sight of the fact that I wanted to paint. Though architecture was in a way related to art, it wasn't really what I wanted to do, it was second best. I love being out of doors, and sometimes I would gaze longingly out of the window at the weather and dream of painting and wonder what on earth I was doing stuck in a stuffy office. Nevertheless, I don't consider those years at all wasted because it was a good discipline and gave me a thorough knowledge of buildings and perspective, which of course now stands me in good stead when painting townscapes and architectural details.

At that time I was still painting mostly in oils, and I began to exhibit with my local art society and with the Royal Institute of Oil Painters at their magnificent old galleries at 195 Piccadilly in London. I also submitted work almost annually to the summer exhibitions at the Royal Academy, but it wasn't until 1973 that I finally had a small oil of a railway siding hung, which was bought by the Japanese Ambassador. By 1964 my work was developing well, I was beginning to get established and was exhibiting more widely. At last I was able to give up architectural work and realize my dream of making a living as a painter. I had married in 1962, and I suppose it was a bit risky giving up a regular job so early in our married life, but things went well and I counted myself very fortunate in being able to do exactly what I wanted to and get paid for it.

By the late 1960s I began to take a greater interest in marine subjects and in 1969 I was invited to join the Wapping Group of Artists, a small art society devoted exclusively to painting the life of the River Thames (more on this in chapter four). I was also elected to the Royal Society of Marine Artists in 1971, and the Royal Institute of Oil Painters in 1972. During these years I travelled extensively around England in search of new subjects to paint, something which I still enjoy doing. We are fortunate, on this tiny island of ours, to have such a varied landscape – and such varied weather conditions! In 1977, I recall, I got the idea to go off for three weeks and do a sort of 'Grand Tour' of the British Isles. It was an idea I'd had in the back of my mind for years, inspired by my first painting trip to Venice and also by the Romantic painters such as Turner and Cozens, who frequently made sketching tours around Britain and much of Europe in the early nineteenth century. I love travelling and discovering new places, and I also relished the thought of spending a few weeks doing nothing else but paint. I suppose painting pictures is no different from playing music, or sport, or dancing: you need time to warm up, to get into your stride, and then you're flying. But if you have to keep stopping, you lose the flow and you are starting from cold again. With none of the distractions of everyday life, such as answering the telephone or getting dragged off to the supermarket, I hoped to be able to produce better work because I could give it my all.

I chose November as potentially the most interesting time of the year in terms of weather and light effects, and I wanted the tour to embrace a variety of subjects, including industrial landscape, some of which is now very threatened and eroded. My route

EVENING STROLL, ALDEBURGH
Watercolour,
$9^1/_2$ x $13^1/_2$in (24x34cm)

took me through the West Country to Wales, then back across to the Midlands and on to the old woollen towns of Yorkshire. By the time I reached Staithes I was beginning to feel exhausted, so I headed for home, stopping off briefly to paint along the coast of East Anglia. I had covered 1,500 miles in nineteen days. The trip was very tiring and taxing (I was ill for two weeks at the end of it), but well worth it; I saw some marvellous sights and managed to produce thirty-eight paintings in oil and watercolour. I exhibited the pictures in London and sold almost all of them. In a way I was sad to see them go as I had put so much of myself into them.

I have painted in every continent except Australia, but it wasn't until 1970 that I first travelled abroad to paint. My first trip was to Venice, in my opinion the most beautiful city in the world. My wife and I had been there on a short holiday in 1966, and I fell instantly in love with it and had to return. And so, four years later, I boarded the *Orient Express* (a sadly neglected old boneshaker in those days) and headed off to spend two weeks exploring and painting the glories of Venice, following in Turner's footsteps. Unlike Turner, however, I painted exclusively in oils on that first trip. Watercolour, more than any other medium, requires practice and dedication; you must really work at it, and at that stage of my career I found I just didn't have the spare time necessary to master the medium.

Opposite
VENETIAN BARGE
Watercolour,
10x6½in (25x16cm)

It is rather sad to think that I have been painting for over fifty years, and yet not until 1974 did I finally made the decision to get to grips with painting in watercolour. During the course of that year virtually every painting I attempted was in watercolour. Through sheer perseverance and much experimenting with different papers and colours, I became acquainted with the way the pigment and water behaved under various conditions. Altogether it took me about a year to complete my watercolour 'apprenticeship' and finally I felt proficient enough to call myself a painter in watercolour as well as oils. I think it was Charlie Chaplin who said 'nobody lives long enough to be anything but an amateur', and I hope that I am still learning and improving. The next picture will always be the best – at least that is what I hope for. Thankfully the success rate improves with experience, but disasters still happen occasionally!

During that year I also studied and analysed the work of my favourite watercolour painters – something I would urge any student of painting to do. Turner, of course, is unrivalled in his depictions of weather, light and atmosphere; I marvel at his ability to convey limitless space with just a drift of watercolour wash. Constable, too, recorded the flickering effects of sun and sky with a freshness and immediacy that could only come from working out of doors, *sur le motif.* In contrast, both Constable and Turner's set-piece works, painted in the studio, leave me cold. I recall seeing John Singer Sargent's watercolours at an exhibition in London and being bowled over by them. I had never seen paintings so fluid and assured, so full of light. I still marvel at them now. The painting *White Ships*, for example, is breathtaking in its evocation of the shifting patterns of light reflected from the water up on to the boat hulls, and I love the way Sargent (1856–1925) used the directional lines of masts and rigging to activate the entire surface of the picture. For quite different reasons, I also admire the work of John Sell Cotman (1782–1842). In contrast to Sargent's bravura style, Cotman constructed his compositions with extreme care and deliberation. Laying down a series of crisp washes, he created an interlocking pattern of colour, line and tone, perfectly balancing one element against another with masterly control. All paintings should have an underlying abstract quality, in other words good design; this is the glue that holds everything together. Cotman's famous painting *Chirk Aqueduct* is a marvellous example of this: the image leaves an indelible imprint on the mind, such is the strength of its abstract design qualities. I find Cotman's work almost before its time in its spare simplicity.

It is a minor tragedy that history has thrown the spotlight on some artists while others equally talented have been pushed into a backwater. In concluding this chapter, then, I would like to mention a largely unknown painter whose work I greatly admire and who I think deserves greater recognition. Harry Becker (1865–1928) dedicated most of his life to portraying the Suffolk landscape and the lives of farm labourers. Becker studied in Paris under the society painter Charles Auguste Emile Carolus-Duran (1838–1917), who taught him the value of confronting nature 'in the raw', and how to paint the landscape with speed, freshness and absolute tonal precision. The key to the latter was first to establish the dominant mid-tone (Carolus-Duran's famous *demi-teinte générale*) and to observe how small were the variations from it necessary to register even extremes of highlight and deep shadow. Becker's paintings evoke a life of toil with remarkable power and dignity and without a trace of sentimentalism, and the energy of his drawing and brushwork expresses a passion, spontaneity and joy in nature which touches me deeply and which I strive to attain in my own work.

Chapter Two

METHODS AND MATERIALS

I am primarily a *plein-air* painter in both oils and watercolour, and my style of handling watercolour is loose and fluid, using what the late Jack Merriott called the 'controlled wash' method. Broadly speaking, this involves establishing the overall tonality and atmosphere of a scene before working up to the details. Much of the picture is completed in a single wash, with the addition of only one or two additional washes to define forms such as trees and buildings. The result is an appearance of cleanliness, translucency and spontaneity. Merriott was a master of this technique and I find it entirely suitable for my purposes in creating atmospheric, predominantly soft-edged paintings.

Like Merriott, I tend to be very purist about using watercolour. I try to use it in the traditional way, without resorting to shortcuts or fancy tricks. For me, the beauty of

LIGHT AND SHADE, SHIRAZ BAZAAR
Watercolour, 21x29in (53x73cm)

watercolour rests in its simplicity and in the delightful transparency of limpid washes of colour which allow the white paper to glow through. I very rarely use body colour, except perhaps when I'm completing a painting back in the studio and need to lighten a small area; in this case I use foundation white, tinted with a little colour. (In my opinion too much body colour can sometimes have a deadening effect, although it depends on the artist.) Occasionally I use a touch of masking fluid, as for example on the tracery of branches in *November Morning, New England* on page 27, but I reserve it only for the absolute highlights. Unless used with restraint, masking fluid can become too obvious; a finished painting should reveal no trace that masking fluid has been used. Once the mask is removed I feather around the hard edges to soften them, and often tint the exposed area with a very weak wash of colour if I feel the white is too stark.

Actually getting started on a painting, being confronted with an intimidating sheet of virgin white paper, is frequently the worst hurdle to get over. More often than not, however, the impact of the subject is such that I can't wait to get going. I tend not to make preliminary sketches because very often there just isn't time – I simply draw on all my senses and get straight on with it. I do, however, assess the subject beforehand in terms of how it will make an interesting composition. The eye level, the light source and the general distribution of tones are essential considerations at this stage. I don't construct these things by rules but by intuition – after a lifetime of painting I just get a feeling when something is right. I usually sketch out the bones of the subject in pencil, but sometimes I simply dampen the paper with a sponge and then float in some weak washes, remembering to leave areas of untouched paper for the extreme lights. I keep everything fluid and loose at this stage, just trying to establish the general atmosphere and tonality of the scene. I like to get the whole sheet covered quickly so as to kill the glaring white of the paper, which is not only intimidating but also gives a false reading of the colours and tones applied in the early stages; these look deceptively strong against the light tone of the paper, but once they are surrounded by adjoining tones and colours it is surprising how much lighter they appear.

I incline my easel at roughly twenty degrees to the horizontal; any greater angle and the washes are apt to drain down to the bottom of the paper, any less and the paint takes longer to dry and is inclined to puddle. I always paint standing up, which allows me (a) to step back frequently to view the painting as a whole, and (b) to paint with my arm rather than working from the wrist. I don't recommend sitting down to paint because you get too comfortable, too sluggish, and it shows in the finished picture. I often see people painting in a relaxed position in a chair (sometimes even a chair with arms!) and I pull their legs about falling asleep on the job. Watercolour painting is like a tightrope walk; as well as physically controlling your washes, you must be continuously aware of the balance of colours and tones as the painting develops because, unlike oils, once you've made a statement it's quite difficult to overcome it. You cannot afford to be relaxed about watercolour painting. I always feel that if I am not completely whacked at the end of a day's painting then I haven't been working at my fullest intensity.

Once the underwash is dry I start working in a more finished way, stressing forms by adding darks or lifting out lights, and maintaining soft edges where I want them. I invariably paint the sky first because this sets the whole key and tone of the picture and influences everything else. I progress from infinity to the foreground and aim to work with no more than one more wash after the initial statement, to maintain the freshness and translucency of the colour. It can be difficult pitching the right tone in watercolour. A mixed wash can appear deceptively strong in a pool on the palette, but of course when it

Above
RETFORD MARKET
Watercolour, 7x10in (18x25cm)

Markets are always lively subjects, and I was particularly taken with this scene in which the colourful, haphazard array of market stalls is set against a backdrop of rather grand Victorian public buildings. It was a bright, breezy morning with a changeable light and there was a lot of movement and activity going on in the market, so I worked rapidly, wet-into-wet, in order to capture the energy of the subject. The feeling of light and life on the ground is echoed in the freely painted sky. The architectural details on the buildings are suggested simply and impressionistically, and I left small chinks of white paper in the initial wash, for example on the slate roofs, to add a degree of sparkle. The breezy, leafless tree on the right stops the eye drifting out of the picture.

Opposite
PIAZZA DELLA REPUBBLICA, FLORENCE
Watercolour, 10x7in (25x18cm)

When out of doors I work on small sheets, usually 7x10in (18x25cm) and occasionally 14x10in (36x25cm), depending on the conditions and the subject. The smaller size is ideal for making a quick statement and allows me to handle the subject within a short time. Piazza della Repubblica, Florence, for example, was a complex architectural subject and I had to paint it quickly before the early morning light changed and the square started to fill with people and traffic. By working on a small sheet and simplifying the subject to its essentials I was able to complete the painting in under an hour.

HIGHCLERE CASTLE
Watercolour,
7x10in (18x25cm)

is spread out thinly on the paper it appears much lighter, and then it dries lighter still. Adding further washes on top to strengthen a tone may disturb the underlayer and turn it muddy. It is important to pitch the tone strong enough at the first attempt since too many superimposed washes, of ill-judged tone and tint, rob the picture of light and purity. An example of a simple, atmospheric subject, handled in just two washes, is *Net Fishing by the Caspian Sea* on page 54.

Finally, I may add some accents of colour and a strong detail here and there, but this is the critical stage when the temptation to start fussing and adding unnecessary details must be resisted. In producing any picture, particularly an involved, complex one, it is sometimes difficult to judge the point when the marks you are making no longer improve the work. You find yourself tinkering and fiddling, and suddenly the freshness has gone and the picture looks laboured. Sometimes I have literally to tell myself out loud, 'stop!' Even so, I do get the odd disaster. Having worked hard and put so much of myself into a painting, contemplating failure can be very discouraging, but there comes a time when I can sense that I'm struggling in vain and that it is pointless to carry on.

I prefer to stop short of finishing absolutely on site. I find it advantageous to reassess the work in the studio the following day and make any final adjustments with the benefit of a fresh eye. Sometimes I may even even decide to retain some simple, unresolved statements which, the previous day, I had thought looked unfinished. I often do a bit of lifting out, with a feather-light touch, to soften an edge here or lighten a tone there. I lightly float some clean water over the area and then use a large, slightly damp brush to gently lift off some of the pigment. This is quite a skilled operation; the paper must be caught when it's beginning to dry – with fully wet paper it is easy to take off more colour than intended or to make streaky marks. Lifting off can only be done over a relatively small area, and there is always the risk of creating a hard edge or bloom as the work dries. As an alternative, I sometimes use a hard eraser when the painting is completely dry to remove some of the pigment in order to lighten an area, but only if I don't intend painting over the area again as the rubbing action scuffs the surface and any subsequent washes are apt to turn muddy.

One tip which I find invaluable is to make a final check of the finished picture by standing with my back to it and viewing it through a small mirror. This has the effect of reversing the image, and any inaccuracies in the drawing or composition are immediately accentuated because I am viewing the picture in an unfamiliar way, almost as an abstract group of shapes.

I painted my very first watercolour (see page 12) on cartridge paper, using student-quality paints and squirrel-hair brushes, but fortunately I soon discovered the benefits of good paper and artists' quality materials. In those days there were some wonderful water-colour papers around which are sadly no longer available. My favourite paper, pre-war Whatman, was so easily available then that I frequently experimented with it in my early efforts. How I wish I had stored it away, unused, until I could paint better! To me, paper is everything. A good paper is a joy to work on, and one feels a certain empathy when painting on a sheet that has just the right texture, weight and degree of sizing. I like to paint on a fairly rough-textured paper; smooth, hot-pressed papers don't suit my way of working. Ideally, the surface should be neither too hard nor too absorbent; if the paper is oversized the paint runs off the surface and when a wash is added the underlayer just lifts off and makes an awful mess. At the other extreme, if the surface is undersized the paint sinks in and it is difficult to vary it or lift it out.

NOVEMBER MORNING, NEW ENGLAND
Watercolour, 7x10in (18x25cm)

I like to experiment with various papers, choosing, for example, a soft paper for a misty scene and a harder, rougher surface for a crisper, livelier subject. I think it's a mistake to stick to one particular paper for all subjects because continual use of something which is safe and familiar breeds complacency. In general I prefer to work on white papers which allow light to reflect off the surface and give the watercolour washes their full and transparent brilliance, but sometimes a subject such as a shadowy interior or a rainy street scene lends itself to the use of a tinted paper. *Prague Town Square* (page 31) was painted on David Cox paper, which has a subtle oatmeal colour and an unusual, slightly fibrous surface. The warmish tint of the paper, left untouched in parts, gives the work a low, harmonious tonality. I am lucky enough to have a stock of old watercolour papers, including some G and M, Russell Flint, RWS, Hayle Mill, Hodgkinson's, Unbleached Arnold, and David Cox. My small stock of pre-war Whatman paper is particularly precious to me, and I use it sparingly. It's a wonderful paper, made from linen rag so the washes flow beautifully and the surface stands up well to washing out and subsequent working on. I'm always on the lookout for old stock, so when I spotted an advertisement in a magazine offering old Whatman paper for sale, my heart leapt. I rang the number and, joy of joys, the chap said it was definitely Whatman paper and yes, it had a textured surface. I immediately arranged to go and see it, though it was quite a journey. The paper was indeed Whatman, but it turned out to be a smooth paper for printing, not painting. Imagine my disappointment! The magic name 'Whatman' had, in the event, sent me on a wild goose chase. Still, it was worth making the effort as I might have been lucky!

I know many artists will share my view that few of the papers available today are as good as the old makes. I'm told it's because papers used to be made from pure linen rag, which is nowadays too rare and expensive and has been substituted by cotton rag and wood pulp. Of the modern papers, I find Arches suits me because it has a good texture and takes washes well, although I find it tends to stain and I have difficulty in lifting some of the colours out. Bockingford has quite a soft surface; it will bear a little lifting out, but if you overwork it it will scuff up the surface. Waterford is slightly harder and is good for painting lively subjects with strong tonal contrasts. I also like Fabriano and Two Rivers.

I normally use a 140lb/300gsm paper, stretched to

COLOURFUL SARIS, UDAIPUR GHATS
Watercolour 21x29in (53x74cm)

Above
GRAVESEND
Watercolour, 7x10in (18x25cm)

It was a rather bleak, grey morning with a few breaks in the cloud cover. For this picture I chose a David Cox paper, whose oatmeal tint would set an overall colour harmony. I managed to position myself behind a wall, which gave me a degree of shelter from the biting wind, and watched for some minutes how the changing patterns of light pierced the cloud cover and reflected off the windswept water. I was interested in the perspective evident in the cloud formations and the way the clouds overlapped each other like a series of stage flats as they receded into the distance. The shapes of the boats seen against the light on the right and the tug towing lighters on the left frame the silhouetted ship moving upstream in the sunlit area. A touch of body colour has been added to accentuate this bright passage of water.

Opposite
PRAGUE TOWN SQUARE
Watercolour, 10x7in (25x18cm)

Another picture painted on David Cox paper, chosen to suggest the warm but overcast light of a cold spring morning. By leaving some areas of the paper untouched, as on the warmer parts of the buildings and the sky, much of the work was done for me and the background colour has a harmonizing influence on the whole picture. It's a pity this paper is no longer available because I find its colour ideal for this sort of subject and I like its unusual, slightly hairy surface. Mind you, it's not an easy paper to use as it is so soft and absorbent. You have to be careful about pitching your tones because when you put a colour on it dries even lighter than it does on other watercolour papers. You also have to remember to state the cooler colours more positively than usual, to compensate for the warm colour of the paper.

T. Chamberlain

avoid cockling. When stretching small sheets I use Sundeala board, which is fairly soft but not as soft as fibreboard. Small sheets of heavier paper, say 200lb/410gsm or more, require no stretching. For stretching larger sheets I use something more substantial such as a drawing board or a thick piece of plywood.

I soak the paper in a sink or bowl for five to ten minutes, depending on the weight and degree of surface sizing; experience will tell you how long a particular paper needs. I remove the sheet and let it drain for a minute or so before securing it to the board. Instead of using strips of gummed tape, I find it easier and quicker to staple round the edges of the paper at about 4in/10cm intervals, using a staple gun. This I find holds the paper in place more securely than gummed tape.

I sometimes use a full imperial (32x21in/81x53cm) sheet when producing a large watercolour in the studio from a small watercolour sketch painted on the spot. In this case I always use a heavy paper (300–400lb/600–850gsm) and I may even stretch it, though it isn't strictly necessary, to be absolutely sure of no cockling in the first wet wash. The advantage of a heavyweight paper is that it stands up to stretching without losing any of its texture.

As with paper, I think one has to use the best quality brushes. I rarely use synthetic brushes as I find they quickly lose their shape. The sable and synthetic mixtures are a little better, but there is no substitute for pure Kolinsky sable brushes. They cost a king's ransom, but they are worth it; with proper care they will last a lifetime, and they have a unique spring and life to them which cheaper brushes always lack. Sables have the capacity to hold a lot of paint and they also taper to a fine point, which means I can switch with ease from laying washes to adding detail, using one brush instead of two.

I do the majority of my work with just three brushes: a No 8, No 12 and No 14 round. For larger paintings I may use a french polisher's mop or a shaving brush to put in the first wash. I also have a ¾in/18mm flat brush, the chisel edge of which is useful for lifting out

TRAM TERMINUS, FLEETWOOD PROMENADE
Watercolour,
7x10in (18x25cm)

EVENING HERTFORD BASIN
Watercolour, 7x10in (18x25cm)

I'm a bit of a perfectionist, but not in the sense of striving for a neatly finished picture. It's just that I won't take second-best, and will destroy a picture if it doesn't convey what originally motivated me to paint the subject. I also take a lot of trouble with getting the balance of shapes, colours and tones right. It can be difficult to assess a painting objectively at the end of a long and tiring session, and I find that taking a fresh look at it the following day helps me to see it more clearly. Looking at this picture in the cold light of day, for example, I decided to darken the trees behind the figures, their reflection in the water, and the surface weed. Just a little thing, but it made all the difference to this area of the painting.

REAR VIEW
Watercolour,
6x10in (15x25cm)

small highlights. A No 4 rigger brush is useful for painting fine details such as fine branches and boat rigging, though I use it sparingly otherwise the painting begins to look more like a drawing. I also keep a small, old brush exclusively for applying masking fluid, thus saving my best brushes from certain ruin.

With regard to paints, I would advocate buying artists' quality over the cheaper student range, even for a beginner just practising. Artists' quality paints give superior results because they flow better and are more luminous. Because they contain more pigment and less binding, making the colours more intense, they go further and therefore are more economical in the long run.

I use both tube and pan colours, though I tend to use tube colour to top up empty pans in my paintbox rather than squeezing them on to a palette. I try to squeeze out just enough paint for my immediate needs because tube colour tends to dry out in the pan if left for a couple of weeks. Then I have to scrub at the paint to get it moving again, which doesn't do much for the state of my brushes!

I look upon myself as primarily a tonal painter with colour in a supporting role. My palette of colours has changed very little over the years and consists a small selection of quiet, restrained hues, which I feel produce a more considered and harmonious result than a riot of intense colours. I use a lot of raw sienna, which looks brown in the palette but dilutes down to a lovely soft, transparent yellow that sympathizes beautifully with other colours in mixes. I prefer it to yellow ochre, which is rather opaque, and cadmium yellow, which is too bright and strident in washes. Olive green is a good all-round green that can be modified with other colours such as burnt sienna and French ultramarine. I also use viridian, a cooler green which can be quite fierce and needs to be used with care. I find that certain makes of viridian tend to dry out very quickly in the paintbox and

THE WHITE KIMONO
Watercolour, 14x10in (35x25cm)

sometimes become grainy in mixes, but I have at last found a really good viridian which retains its fluidity well, made by Talens. Likewise, alizarin crimson must be used sparingly; it is transparent but staining. Recently I've taken to using permanent magenta instead as it is a softer colour. I also use burnt sienna and burnt umber, and Venetian red is useful sometimes for painting buildings. Cobalt blue is quite expensive, but I like its softness when painting skies. French ultramarine is a good standby blue, and when used on a rough paper can give a pleasing granulated effect. I avoid strong blues such as Prussian or Winsor as they're so fierce and staining and powerful. I also keep the cadmiums – red, yellow and orange – up my sleeve for when I need a bright accent.

I never use black as I feel it makes dark 'holes' in a picture, although it can be mixed with raw sienna or certain yellows to make interesting greens. I find that a mixture of burnt umber and cobalt blue makes a good strong dark with plenty of life in it. There is, of course, no actual black in the landscape as every object is seen through a film of atmosphere and is influenced by the colours of the things around it.

My paints are always arranged in the same order, so that I can go directly to a colour without having to think about it (the only drawback being that I often cannot recall afterwards exactly which colours I mixed for a particular wash as it was done semi-consciously). At one end are the yellows, followed by the greens, blues, reds and then the earth colours.

I treated myself to a brand new paintbox recently. I was quite fond of my old one, but its paint wells were too shallow and it had a flat mixing area, so paint would run all over the place. Then one day my friend and fellow artist David Curtis told me about Craig Young in Cheshire, who makes wonderful paintboxes. The design is based on the old Binning Munro box which was discontinued some years ago, and because Young's boxes are handmade, they can be produced to the customer's specific requirements. For years I have scoured auctions and junk shops in the vain hope of finding a Binning Munro, which to my mind was the perfectly designed watercolour box. At last I have found the nearest equivalent which, though expensive, has proved invaluable. Fashioned from lacquered brass, the box unfolds to reveal generous wells and plenty of mixing recesses.

As a seasoned *plein-air* painter, my advice is to travel light when working out of doors. When trekking across country in search of a suitable subject, you don't want to be encumbered with the entire contents of your studio. I carry a lightweight sketching easel, and the rest of my equipment fits into a canvas shoulder bag. Typically, the bag will contain a lightweight board and half a dozen 7x10in (18x25cm) sheets of unstretched heavyweight papers of various kinds (so that I can choose the best surface for a particular subject or light effect). Then there's my paintbox, plus a metal box containing my brushes, a couple of pencils, hard and soft erasers, a few spare tubes of paint, a small bottle of masking fluid and an old paintbrush for applying it with, and a small natural sponge for lifting out and general wetting and cleaning up. I have a plastic water jar with a handle, which I hang from my easel, and a plastic water bottle. I like to replenish my water jar often while painting, otherwise there is a danger that the colours begin to lose their clarity, brilliance and strength. Last but not least is my trusty spiral-bound sketchbook – an essential item. In bright conditions I find an umbrella useful to keep the sun off the paper when I'm working. I have pierced the spike and inserted a ring so that I can hang it up and work beneath it.

In the end, no amount of equipment or methodology can turn you into an artist. Preoccupation with techniques and materials is really only a protection against inability to see. There is no substitute for actually painting and gaining experience of using watercolour. That and finding your own way and discovering your own signature so that you don't just end up emulating somebody else. Whilst other painters may be admired, and even inspire you, you must discover your own way of working.

In my case, it's interesting that some of the watercolourists I most admire, such as Hercules Brabazon, Albert Goodwin and of course the great Turner, worked in very unconventional ways and yet I myself have always preferred to paint in the traditional, transparent way. These watercolour masters often used tinted papers, employing a combination of watercolour, opaque body colour, pen and ink, chalk, pastel and gum, and wiped out or scratched out with a blade, sponge, rag, fitch brush or sandpaper; yet their paintings have an exquisite freshness and luminosity. Turner's and Goodwin's pictures seem to glow with an inner intensity, conveying the misty shimmer of blue hazy dawns, sombre twilights and burning sunsets. Brabazon was a master at the art of suggestion. He always worked on the spot and is reputed to have spent no more than half an hour on even his most ambitious pictures, often working simultaneously with body colour and watercolour on the same brush to create what Sickert called 'the most fleeting and exquisite surprises of colour'. Brabazon was himself a great admirer of Turner, but he was also an example of how an artist can be inspired by another without becoming a copyist.

As I have said, although I enjoy and respect such painters, I have no desire to ape their techniques – I just want to paint like me, and that's important for any painter. For me, the joy of the fluid wash, fresh and simple and transparent, is what appeals. But what does strike a chord with me about such painters, and is something I try to emulate in my own way, is their ability to go beyond the mere physical representation of a scene to convey the intangibles of light and sun and air and mist. There are many ways in which to exploit the joy of the watercolour medium, but in the end it is not technique which matters but the artist's personal vision.

Opposite
FELUCCA JOURNEY, EGYPT
Watercolour,
14x10in (35x25cm)

T. Chamberlain 1993

Chapter Three

LANDSCAPES

By inclination I am a morning person, and one of my enduring delights is going out to paint very early on a Sunday morning in September when the atmosphere is still misty and hazy. To witness that early bloom, with the air like champagne and the sun shining on the dew-kissed gossamer clothing the meadows, is an exhilarating experience. Objects in the landscape are indistinct and half-seen, reduced to mysterious, tantalizing shapes moving and disappearing into the mellow haze. All the people and cars are still asleep, and the only sound is perhaps the soft cooing of a wood pigeon in the distance. I'm normally quite a placid soul, but these are the conditions I find most exciting and I can't wait to get started, knowing that that magical moment is so transient and that in an hour or so it will all have dissipated.

Painting is all about loving something – a place, an atmosphere, a mood. That first vital impulse to paint, what Bonnard called 'the first seduction', is the most important thing. For me, the first seduction is always light and atmosphere – in fact it is almost an obsession. I'm sure this stems from my being born and brought up in the English countryside; as with all painting, I think one responds most fully and deeply to the things one has observed and lived with over a long period, and I have become highly sensitive to the subtleties and almost imperceptible changes which occur in the landscape under the fickle English weather. Over the years I have done countless paintings of the marshes near our home – indeed my wife Elaine claims that we only moved to this part of Hertfordshire for the marsh mists! I count myself extremely fortunate that I can step out of my front door and find a subject to paint within a matter of minutes. There's a never-ending source of material here – the river, the meadows and the stands of graceful poplar trees which are a feature of the Hertfordshire landscape – but possibly what attracts me most is the particular quality of the light, especially when the river throws up an early morning mist. I have painted the place in all seasons and all weathers and I expect I shall go on doing so until I am ready to drop off my perch.

For me, convincing landscape paintings can only be achieved by working directly from nature on site. Painting isn't just about recording a scene, it's about expressing one's emotional response to the subject and conveying something of that emotion to the viewer. To do that with conviction we need to be there, experiencing the subject at first hand, absorbed in its particular qualities of light, mood, atmosphere, colour and so on. An unseen hand seems to be guiding you when painting nature 'in the raw'. Somehow, when you can hear the lapping of the water, feel the breeze on your face and smell the sweet grass, something of the atmosphere rubs off on you and this fosters an intensive response which in turn helps to produce a painting that is fresh and alive.

Painting in the great outdoors does have its pitfalls, of course, among them having to contend with changing light, uncertain weather, insects and so on. And inevitably, even if you set up your easel in the middle of a field miles from civilization, some well-meaning person will materialize from nowhere, amble up to you and start wittering on about their

MARSH MIST, WATERFORD
Watercolour, 9½x13½in (24x34cm)

This is one of the many paintings I have done on the marsh that lies just a short walk from my house. The river that runs across the marsh sometimes throws up a mist that shrouds the whole valley and turns it into a place of magic and mystery. I painted this very early on a September morning, with the sun just beginning to glow through the mist. I chose a viewpoint looking directly into the light so as to emphasize the aerial perspective of the silhouetted shapes receding into the distant haze.

A subject like this may at first glance appear fairly monochromatic, but you have to be aware of the subtle changes of tone and colour and avoid reducing everything to a series of flat washes. Here, for example, I was careful to make the sky lighter and warmer on the left, where the sun was strongest, and to record the warm and cool sides of the trees.

grandson or their auntie who paints. Some artists I know are very good at dealing with inquisitive onlookers and bear their interruptions with good grace, but I like to immerse myself completely in my painting and hate to be disturbed. In order to discourage any attempts at conversation I employ a number of defence strategies, including clenching a brush between my teeth, or flicking a loaded brush on the ground, so forcing onlookers to step back – oh, and I have a bad habit of sucking my brush to dry it, and then I spit rather than swallow. That certainly puts them off! If I'm painting with a group and encounter a persistent character, I can be cheeky and say, 'I should go and see that fella over there, he's a much better painter than me.'

However, such problems are minor compared with the pleasure of being in direct contact with nature. To be 'fired' by the subject, and experience the urgency of responding equally to the changing moods of nature and to events on the paper, heightens the senses and gives impetus to one's work. Of course, such tunnel vision can sometimes be dangerous, too. I remember one occasion when I was so fired up about a frosty landscape at dawn that, on moving back to review my progress, I stepped backwards into the river. Luckily it was quite shallow, but it was jolly cold! And when I painted *Shadow Patterns on the Sails, Aswan* (opposite) on an island on the Nile, my colleagues and I were so immersed in the beauty of the scene that we quite forgot the time and were late in leaving.

HEAT HAZE, GIZA
Watercolour, 7x10in (18x25cm)

SHADOW PATTERNS ON THE SAILS, ASWAN
Watercolour, 9$\frac{3}{4}$x13$\frac{1}{4}$in (24x33cm)

I love these small sailing boats, called feluccas, which ply the waters around Africa and the Mediterranean. With their wing-like sails they look like delicate butterflies sitting on the water. We hired a felucca to take us across from Aswan to a small island on the Nile. It was early evening and warm sunlight was filtering through a bank of trees near the shore, casting lovely shadow patterns on to the sparkling white sails of two feluccas moored near by. I was fascinated by these patterns, so delicate and luminous, and I wanted to make them the focus of my painting, so in the interests of making a better composition I 'moved' the boats further out into the river so that I could give full prominence to the sails. Their shapes are lovely in themselves, and the way they are juxtaposed, forming a deep V-shape against the sky, makes for an arresting composition.

EARLY LIGHT, ABU SIMBEL
Watercolour, 10x14in (25x35cm)

The wind had dropped, so to get away from the island I had to use my easel to paddle us out to midstream, where we were lucky enough to pick up a breath of wind. Once at the other side I proffered my hat to the two Egyptian boatmen and asked for 'baksheesh', but to no avail.

When out on location I often walk around for a while, absorbing the atmosphere of the place and assessing the light and weather. I like to be surprised by turning a corner and seeing a potential subject rather than setting out to find something specific. However, time is a key factor in an outdoor situation and once I have determined my subject I find it is essential to start painting without delay. There may well be a more exciting idea around the next corner, but vital painting time can be lost trying to hunt out the 'perfect' subject. Besides, it is not always the subject itself that appeals but the way it is transformed by light and weather. The best works have a certain poetry which speaks to you. It could be something as simple as the dappled shadow patterns cast on to a wall by nearby trees, or the early morning sun filtering through the mist, or the translucent glow of backlit evening clouds.

Often it's a question of being in the right place at the right time; it's no good making a note of a place and thinking 'I must come back and paint here sometime'. It may work out, but very often you are disappointed because when you return the light might be very different, and you wonder what you saw in the subject before. The key is to seize the moment. I remember when I painted *Early, Still Morning on the Nile* (page 53) I had only just finished painting and was packing up when an enormous tourist boat moored at the quay right in front of me and obliterated my view. I was so glad I had wasted no time in capturing the subject; had I dithered about what to paint, this catastrophe could well have happened when I was in the middle of the painting.

Whenever I find a good subject I enjoy returning to it again and again and painting it from a number of viewpoints at different times of the day and in various climatic conditions, just as Monet did. I would advise anyone painting landscapes to do the same; the insights gained from painting regularly at a few locations will help you to cope when you find yourself working in unfamiliar places. The three paintings overleaf demonstrate various interpretations of the same subject. Budleigh Salterton, on the south Devon coast, is a favourite painting spot of mine; approaching the town from the east, you round a corner at the top of the cliff and suddenly this stunning view is revealed like a vast cinema screen. Whenever I visit the area I look forward eagerly to turning that corner because I never know what to expect; obviously the coastal features themselves remain the same, but the weather, the light and the atmosphere are constantly changing and the effects are often spectacular.

HOT SUMMER EVENING, HERTINGFORDBURY
Watercolour, 7x10in (18x25cm)

Above
HEAVY CLOUD, BUDLEIGH SALTERTON
Watercolour, 7x10in (18x25cm)

This painting and its companions opposite demonstrate the value of returning to a subject and painting it under different climatic conditions and from different viewpoints.

This small study was painted on the spot, with a few minor adjustments made back in the studio. I liked the way the heavy clouds seemed to be pressing down on the cliff, and the contrast of the dark background with the bright foreground, eerily lit by a sudden shaft of sunlight. It was a frenzied effort as the weather and the light were so changeable. In my haste I have created a few 'blooms' in the sky and sea – happy accidents that add texture and movement.

Opposite, top
RAIN, BUDLEIGH SALTERTON
Watercolour, 20x28in (51x71cm)

The rain was coming down in sheets, so I made a small watercolour sketch from the shelter of my car and used it as reference for this large studio painting. I used a heavyweight Fabriano rough paper, which keeps its texture well and doesn't cockle under heavy washes.

Opposite, bottom
HAZE, BUDLEIGH SALTERTON
Watercolour, 7x10in (18x25cm)

This was painted, believe it or not, in high summer! The atmosphere was so delicate and subtle, with the warmth of the sun filtering through the cool mist, and I liked the heightened aerial perspective of the cliffs gradually disappearing into the hazy distance. A peach of a subject, with the clusters of buildings, boats and figures lending scale and life and helping to anchor the composition.

T. Chamberlain

T. Chamberlain '93.

In choosing a viewpoint, protecting your work from the weather is paramount. In bright conditions I always try to work in the shade or, failing that, I position my easel so that the light strikes the paper from right or left. If the sun shines directly on to the paper not only will washes dry out too quickly, but back in the studio the picture dies. The glare of sunshine on white paper is very uncomfortable and gives the washes a false sense of warmth because it tires the eyes and dulls one's sense of colour. Keeping out of the wind is also a good idea; with too much flapping of paper it is difficult to control your work.

Watercolour is more difficult to handle than oils in adverse conditions. On a damp, drizzly day washes refuse to dry and rain-spots are apt to ruin your crucial first wash; on a frosty winter morning, washes can actually freeze on the paper; and in hot, dry conditions the washes dry too quickly and unwanted marks and streaks appear where one wash begins to dry before the next one is placed. Some of these problems can be overcome, however, with a little ingenuity. On a misty day I simply turn my painting to the sun, if there is any, to dry; alternatively, I give it a quick blast with a tiny hairdryer which I plug into the cigar lighter in my car. I have also heard that a few drops of gum arabic added to the water jar helps to prevent washes drying too quickly in the heat of summer, while a drop of gin similarly applied will keep washes from freezing on the paper in winter. (I must try that one some day.) Otherwise, it's a question of assessing the conditions before you begin and avoiding difficult ones if you feel you will be fighting a losing battle.

In my experience the most rewarding time to paint, especially in hot countries, is either early morning or late afternoon and evening as the conditions tend to be more settled then and are more conducive to laying in washes. Between six and eight in the morning there is a fresh bloom in the air and the lighting effects can be remarkable, especially in spring and autumn. Another advantage is that there are fewer people and cars around at that time of the day. In the evening, when the heat of the day is less, colours are warmer and the shadows lengthen. Of course, there is the problem of a rapidly

BRIGHT DAY, GREENWICH WATERFRONT
Watercolour, 10½x21in (26x53cm)

FIRST SNOW OF THE WINTER
Watercolour,
7x10in (18x25cm)

fading light, but if you are very fast you could even tackle that magical period of twilight. Twilight painting is not for the faint hearted as it only lasts about twenty minutes, but it's usually enough to get something of the mood down on paper. The next morning you can assess your effort and refine it, while your memory is still fresh.

I am definitely a slave to the weather. Before I go out for a day's painting, I listen intently to the weather forecast, tap fretfully at the barometer and look up at the weathercock atop the church next door to our house, and I still can't decide whether or not to risk going out. I don't know why I worry so much; in Britain, if you always wait for warm sunny weather to come along you won't get much painting done. Besides, fine paintings can be executed even in dull weather, as demonstrated by my fellow-artist David Curtis, who manages to breathe a marvellous outdoor feeling into his work, often produced under the sullen skies of his native Yorkshire. It's a bit of a national pastime to bemoan the British weather, but as an artist I think we are lucky to experience such a diversity of conditions: sun, rain, snow, fog, hail, wind and frost – sometimes all in one day!

I enjoy the changing of the seasons, too. Spring is so fresh and invigorating and the atmosphere crisp and bright, although somewhat saturated with greens. Early spring is the best time, when the trees are still almost bare, with patches of new leaves showing in places. High summer has a more settled atmosphere, but a bout of hot weather can be suddenly shattered by a thunderstorm, itself an exciting subject. Strong sunshine produces a wider range of tones, colours are intensified and there can be lovely deep shadows and rich greens, with strong contrasts of warm and cool colour. Autumn at its best can be truly a season of mists and mellow fruitfulness, with a wonderful warm light and atmosphere. This is perhaps my favourite season for handling watercolour, when I can really let the washes flow and capture the impression of the landscape dissolved in mist and haze. I avoid painting the excessive fiery tints of massed autumn foliage, preferring instead late November, when there are just a few straggly groups of leaves remaining. Winter can be a very rewarding time to paint if you can overcome the hardships of painting outdoors. The sun is much lower in the sky, there is a cold stillness to the atmosphere and there are wonderful subtle colours and tones, particularly in the sky, when a sudden flash of creamy pink near the horizon can transform an otherwise ordinary landscape.

Skies are an ever-changing source of material which constantly inspires me. Cloud effects can change shape very quickly, and I find the fluidity, speed and directness of watercolour enables a fast and direct response. The sky dictates the mood of a scene, and is undoubtedly the single most influential element. Whilst being all air and vapour it still has form, tone, colour, and linear and aerial perspective. So often pictures are seen with rather nondescript, 'formula' watercolour skies, fluidly painted but without any true reference to cloud formations and perspective.

The first priority when painting skies is to determine the direction of the light. The sky near the sun has an influence of warm yellow, and becomes darker and cooler further away. In bright conditions the shapes of cumulus clouds are clearly defined by the contrast of light and dark on their rounded forms. If the sun is behind you, you will see light-coloured cloud shapes with shadows to the undersides. When seen against the light, the clouds may appear as dark shapes with light shining through them, sometimes with 'silver linings' around the edges. When clouds are broken, be aware of the way they overlap and become smaller, flatter and more closely spaced as they recede towards the horizon. Clouds in the distance lose definition and blend into the mistiness of aerial atmosphere.

After sponging the paper I indicate light sides of the clouds with a weak wash of raw sienna; I tend not to leave areas of pure white paper, except for really bright highlights, as I find the effect too stark. While the paper is still wet, I work in the warm, dark tones on the shadow sides with raw sienna, burnt sienna and cobalt in various degrees from warm to cool. At this stage it's important to keep it fluid and flowing and not become too involved in delineating form. At the same time you must control the degree of wetness in the washes, otherwise the paint flows all over the place and you lose control. Finally, I float in the darkest areas with burnt sienna and cobalt blue, with perhaps a touch of red or green, depending on the conditions.

It is tempting to overstate the blue of a summer sky and make it too bright, so that the luminous, aerial quality is lost and the sky comes forward like a wall. Even on a cloudless day the sky is not just an unbroken sheet of blue but contains many subtle variations in colour. It is warmest at the zenith, then turns gradually lighter and cooler as it recedes. Close to the horizon it takes on a warm, pearly quality with a yellow, pink or even ochre hue, where it is seen through the thicker atmosphere. This is particularly noticeable at dusk. When painting blue skies I first dampen the surface and apply a pale band of raw sienna over the lower sky area and overlay this with a graduated wash of cobalt blue, possibly modified with burnt sienna to soften it, and making it slightly darker at the top of the sky. Near the horizon I might apply a faint flush of burnt sienna or alizarin crimson. To establish of feeling of misty haze in the distance I take my washes down over

SHEEP IN A FROSTY MEADOW
Watercolour, 7x10in (18x25cm)

I love the transient aspects of the English weather, and in particular hazy sunlight and mists. The whole concept of this picture is fairly simple, with a straightforward composition and a limited colour scheme of soft yellows, blues and greys. This play of warm and cool gives the idea of a frosty, but bright, sunny morning. I have tried to get the feeling of light behind the tree by putting on an initial wash of light, warm colour and then painting the silhouette over it. There is a pleasing counterchange of lights and darks: the sheep seen against the light on the left appear quite dark, the light just catching their backs, while those under the tree appear quite light against the dark shadows. I dampened the ground on which the sheep are standing so that their legs appear to melt into the mist.

the distant horizon and allow them to blend wet-into-wet with the landscape wash. Abutting washes along the horizon creates a hard line which kills the feeling of one thing being behind another in space.

When observing the gradations of the sky's mantle, I find it helpful to tilt my head 90 degrees to one side so that I am looking at the sky from an unfamiliar, sideways angle. The subtle changes in the sky are somehow seen more clearly this way, and I have long since accustomed myself to the quizzical glances of onlookers when I do this. I also compare the relative tonal values between the clouds, sky and landscape. Concentrating for too long on the clouds makes them appear darker than they actually are, resulting in a heavy sky that lacks airiness and luminosity.

Skies change and develop quickly, even in relatively settled conditions, and it is tempting forever to chase the next interesting effect that comes along. This is a mistake of course, and invariably leads to confusion and muddiness. Rather than trying to include everything, it is best to focus only on the most interesting part of the sky and put it in immediately. Fix the main cloud shapes first and simplify their shape and number. With experience your visual memory develops and you are able to hold an image in your head even after it has changed or disappeared. As your painting progresses, bring sky and landscape along at the same rate. Both must be perfectly related and in harmony with each other. Clouds often cast shadows on to the landscape below and these must be

Opposite
CHANGEABLE WEATHER, WIVENHOE
Watercolour, 7x10in (18x25cm)

I was on a painting trip to the river Colne with the Wapping Group, and the weather that day was indeed changeable, with squally rain one minute and bright sunshine the next. When this interesting formation of clouds came along I seized on them and got them down quickly before they sailed off. I decided to make a feature of the clouds, arranging them to overlap with the church bell tower, suggesting a 'C' shaped format with the saltings in the foreground. Enclosed within this shape is the focal point, the sunlit cluster of buildings and the berthed vessel. I have simplified the background to a simple dark shape, steeped in cloud shadow, so as not to compete with the buildings along the wharf.

Above
BOWLS, SIDMOUTH
Watercolour, 10x14in (25x35cm)

There's a sparkling quality to the light at the seaside - it bounces everywhere, giving solid forms a light, airy feel. I revelled in recording the subtle nuances of light, shadow and reflected light in this scene, particularly on the billowing clouds, the white buildings and the white-clad figures. There are slabs of strong, direct light on the slate roofs, the walls in shadow are cool and translucent, and the gable ends between the buildings are lit by warm reflected light from the walls opposite them, which face the sun. Notice how the shadows on the upper parts of the figures are sharp and cool, while those lower down are more diffused and warmed by light reflected from the ground.

T. Chamberlain 1993.

EARLY, STILL MORNING ON THE NILE
Watercolour, $10^1/_4$ x $14^1/_4$in (26x36cm)

As the saying goes: 'the early bird catches the worm'. Having got up at 6am to go in search of a painting subject, this was my reward; a heartbreakingly beautiful view of the Nile. The water was as calm as a mill pond, the air had a soft mistiness to it, and the grouping of the little jetty and the boats, together with their reflections, made a nice shape against the smooth expanse of sky and water. I composed the picture so that this would form the focal point, positioned one third of the way across the sheet.

I wanted to capture the absolutely still, calm atmosphere of early morning, so I stuck to a limited palette of raw sienna, burnt sienna, cobalt blue and a few touches of olive green. I also simplified some of the detail and painted most of the picture with soft, limpid washes applied wet-into-wet.

NET FISHING
BY THE CASPIAN SEA
Watercolour,
7x10in (18x25cm)

logical in relation to the light source. The introduction of cloud shadows gives a feeling of movement and changing light, and offers compositional opportunities because the eye is naturally drawn to where darks and lights meet.

Lakes, rivers, streams and ponds are attractive but elusive subjects. Ripples and eddies come and go; colours change; reflections break and re-form. It goes without saying that watercolour's transparency, fluidity and speed are ideally suited to this aspect of the landscape. Just as when painting skies, it is important to compare the relative tonal values, both within the various parts of the water itself and between the water, the sky and the land. The surface of a large expanse of calm water will reflect the sky almost exactly, although in a slightly muted way. The further away the water surface is, the lighter and more influenced by the sky it is, and the surface may be scuffed by the breeze.

Depending on the clarity and local colour of the water, the reflections of dark colours appear lighter, and light colours appear darker. Before you start to paint, take the time to study the ripples and reflections and try to fix them in your mind's eye. Analyse the most important shapes in the water and paint them swiftly and simply. Convey the still surface of a lake or river with broad washes on wet paper, letting your brush strokes settle undisturbed. Dragging a semi-dry brush of colour across dry, rough-textured paper is a wonderfully economical means of suggesting spangles of light on the water or a wind-ruffled surface. Ripples and reflections can be described in a kind of shorthand with

THAMES REFLECTIONS
Watercolour,
$7^1/_4$ x $10^1/_4$in (19x26cm)

wavering lines and calligraphic squiggles, letting the action of your brush suggest the water's undulating movement.

Trees are a prominent element in most landscapes, but they are usually seen from a distance and so it is more important to convey their overall shape than to paint them in detail. It is always necessary to simplify to some extent, whether you are painting bare winter trees or foliage-clad summer ones. Look for the large shapes and masses that characterize the tree and block these in broadly before starting to pick out any details. Even less detail is needed for trees in the distance, although one should beware of painting them with a single flat wash; subtle modulations of tone and of warm and cool colour will give a more atmospheric effect.

Be aware that a tree is not just a flat shape but has three-dimensional form. Keep in mind the direction of the light and use light and shade to define the volume of trunks, branches and clumps of foliage. Note how branches extend towards you and away from you as well as from side to side, and look for lighter areas of foliage which may occur in front of the trunk. Careful observation will show you that the light side of a tree picks up warm colours, whereas the shadow side contains hints of cool blue and violet and may also pick up reflected light from the surroundings. Note also how tree trunks usually get darker as they rise up into the shadows of the leaf masses, but are lighter nearer the ground, where they are influenced by reflected light and colour.

SHEEP ON THE MEADS, HERTFORD
Watercolour, 7x10in (18x26cm)

A successful composition combines harmony and restraint with enough diversity to keep the eye entertained. In this scene, the two trees echo each other but one is taller than the other and one is in sunlight, the other in shade. Similarly the cumulus clouds find an echo in the rounded forms of the sheep, which I have arranged in groups that lead the eye through the picture. Note, too, the rhythmic repetition of warm and cool colour in the sky, the distant hills, the sunlit field and the foreground shadow.

SHADE, PRAGUE CASTLE
Watercolour, 7x10in (18x25cm)

Hard outlines make trees look one-dimensional, so I usually dampen the paper around the edges of the tree shape before painting it so that the colour just bleeds gently into the surrounding sky with a soft, feathery edge. This helps to express the idea of the tree as a living, animate thing and to integrate it with the surrounding atmosphere. Except in the distance, even when a tree is in full foliage there are always little 'sky holes' within the canopy, especially around the edges, so allow for these when putting in your initial wash and skip the brush around so as to leave tiny chinks of white paper.

In very bright conditions there will be a lot of strong, sharp-edged shadows, but on an overcast day they tend to be paler and softer. Look for reflected light bouncing into the shadows from the sky or from nearby objects. This is an important factor in creating atmosphere and luminosity in your paintings. The further a shadow is from the object casting it, the softer it will be. Think of the shadow cast by a tree, for instance: the part nearest the trunk is sharpest and the further it travels from the tree the paler and softer it becomes, because more light is reflected into it from the sky.

Similarly, if you look at the shadow on a wall you will see that it is lighter at the base where light from the ground is bouncing up into it. To achieve this effect I normally dampen the outer edges of the shadow and allow the shadow wash to fade out wet-into-wet. The shadows in *Shadow Patterns on the Sails, Aswan* (page 41) have a delicate lost-and-found quality and are tinged by the warmth of the evening light. To capture this effect I wetted the paper and dropped in some warm colour around the edges of the shadow shapes. When this was almost dry I put in the cooler main body of the shadow. Notice also how the shadow appears darker when seen against the sky, becoming lighter and warmer further down.

Nature is bountiful, and when painting on site there is a tendency to include too much detail 'because it's there'. Simplicity is a key element in good composition; a painting is a distillation of nature, and all the more powerful for that. Try to see the landscape in terms of broad masses rather than a collection of little bits. Look at the subject through half-closed eyes as this will eliminate detail and help you to see the tonal areas in relation to one another. Concentrate on the thing that drew you to the scene in the first place and suppress the desire to put in that other attractive feature which you've just noticed – it will only confuse the compostion.

Very rarely will a scene appear before you already perfectly composed. In most cases you will have to rearrange at least slightly, perhaps omitting a tree, or lowering the horizon so as to accentuate the sky. *Early, Still Morning on the Nile* (page 53) was a simple subject, but I simplified it even more in order to express the atmosphere of quiet calm. There was another boat in the foreground, which I edited out as I wanted to play off the visual calm of the water on the right of the picture against the activity on the left. I also simplified the background and positioned the small white felucca in the distance to give a sense of depth and act as a counterpoint to the large, dark mass in the foreground.

THE FALL, BOSTON
Watercolour, 7x10in (18x25cm)

FISHING BY THE RIVER LEA
Watercolour,
7x10in (18x25cm)

The spirit of a place will not necessarily be lost by such pruning and transplanting – indeed it will more likely be enhanced. Nature often needs a little assistance from the artist to express or accentuate her beauty. The late playwright Bernard Miles once related a story of a passer-by complimenting a gardener on his beautiful flower garden, saying, 'It's wonderful what God can do in a garden with a little help'. The gardener replied, 'Yes, you should have seen the state of it when He had it to himself'. I think the same applies to a landscape; you just can't take it as it is, you must make it into something yourself.

Planning a composition in watercolour is like planning a military campaign; you must be disciplined and have a clear plan of action before you start painting, otherwise you will be fighting a losing battle. You must know where the lightest and darkest tones are going to be, and since the brightest lights are provided by the white of the paper, you need constantly to hold back, resisting the temptation to fill them in. You must be aware of the consequences of each move you make, asking questions like 'While I'm doing this, how can I maintain that?' and 'If I put in a dark here, how is that going to affect the balance of the composition?'

All the time the effects of light and shadow must be kept in mind, for not only do these give a sense of space and support the composition, they also convey mood and atmosphere. Use shadows creatively in your compositions. Cast shadows help to describe the form of objects they fall across, and patterns of light and shadow moving through the

LATE AFTERNOON, COVERACK
Watercolour, 7x10in (18x25cm)

This scene stopped me in my tracks – a ready-made composition, simple yet arresting. I love the inherent stability of the interlocking triangular shapes – of the roofs and chimneys, the patterns of light and shadow and the trapped shape of the sea. I knew it was going to be a race against time as I could see that clouds were beginning to creep up from the southwest, but I thought I could at least get a small painting done. I got as far as laying in the first washes when the clouds came up and I lost the light completely. However, I was undefeated because I had managed to get the ghost of the image down and had nailed the approximate tones and colours and the positions of the shadows. Thus I was able to complete the painting by holding the original image in my head.

landscape will also serve as a linking passage to help the composition. Where you have, for instance, an empty road in a picture, a shadow falling across it will enliven it and lead the eye across the picture. A dark shadow in the foreground will frame and accentuate a well-lit centre of interest.

No matter how well it is drawn and painted, or how good the colour and tonal harmonies are, if a picture is badly composed it will be so much wasted effort. A well-composed picture fits together in a satisfying way even though we may not be able to explain exactly why. An interesting division of space is important, and various pictorial arrangements can be applied, including circular, rectangular, triangular, diagonal, radiating, L-shaped and S-shaped divisions. All good paintings have underlying abstract qualities, with light and dark, line and mass, rhythms and emphases all working together to entice the eye around the picture and guide it to the main area of interest, which itself is carefully placed for balance and maximum visual impact.

Look for lines or implied lines such as roads, hedges and cloud formations that follow through and link areas. Look also for the counterchange of light objects against dark, and dark against light, which enlivens the composition and also helps to create the impression of one object being in front of another. Introduce contrasts and echoes of shape, tone and colour to give both harmony and visual interest. Be aware of balance, but in an asymmetrical way so as to avoid boredom; if there is a large shape in the left foreground, place something small in the right background to balance it. Avoid having a passage of loud unrelated colour or an area of strong tone badly placed at the edge of a picture. I could go on, but I'm sure most of you are already familiar with compositional guidelines such as these, and they are largely a matter of common sense. With experience you will learn to trust your instincts rather than becoming hidebound by geometry.

Aerial perspective, which describes the modulation of tone and hue from foreground to infinity, is the single most important factor in achieving atmosphere and giving the effect of recession. Certainly the effect is most obvious in conditions such as fog, rain or

EARLY BIRDS
Watercolour,
14x21½in (35x54cm)

PUDDLE IN THE ROAD
Watercolour, 7x10in (18x25cm)

heat haze, but even on a bright spring day or after a sharp shower of rain, when the air is crisp and lucid, aerial perspective can still be discerned. In my first overall wash I try to pitch the tone and colour accurately as some of this will remain as part of my final statement. From the palest shapes on the horizon to the darkest darks in the foreground, all the tonal and colour relationships must be accurately observed so that everything is in its correct place; if a distant object or area is too dark or prominent it can throw the whole thing out of key.

After many years of constantly looking hard and training my eye, I am now highly attuned to the subtle nuances of tone, colour and edge quality that lend a feeling of light and atmosphere to a painting. I have seen so many otherwise excellent watercolours that have a slightly flinty, unyielding quality because the artist has given everything in the picture too much definition and failed to observe the way light defines some shapes and dissolves others. One must also beware of superficial effects, such as painting a distant bank of trees with just a flat wash of blue; on a sunny day there are often barely discernible changes of tone and colour even in the far distance, and the observation of such subtle details lends integrity to a painting.

Chapter Four

MARINE AND COASTAL

Harbour, coastal and estuary scenes have always held a great fascination for me, and we artists in the British Isles are fortunate in having a long and varied coastline to draw upon. Since my youth I have enjoyed sketching and painting coastal scenes, particularly in south Devon and along the creeks and estuaries of East Anglia, but it wasn't until I was invited to join the Wapping Group of Artists in 1969 that I increased my repertoire and knowledge of maritime subjects. Founded in 1946 in a pub in Wapping, east London, the Group is probably the last proper artists' society left in England. Its sole purpose is to depict the life of the River Thames, from its tranquil upper reaches, through London and down to the wide expanses of the Kent and Essex coast. We are a small confraternity of twenty-five painters who meet regularly each Wednesday during the spring and summer months at an agreed spot along the Thames for a day's painting, followed by a convivial drink at a local hostelry. Not only is it a pleasure to meet up with friends, to paint together and exchange ideas, it is also good discipline, giving me the impetus I need to make the effort to journey to London each week with all my painting gear.

RIVER BUS, BELOW TOWER BRIDGE
Watercolour, 6¾ x 9¾in (17x24cm)

A CLUSTER OF LIGHTERS, RIVER THAMES
Watercolour, 21x28in (53x71cm)

It's very thrilling to see an array of Thames lighters and barges such as this. The boats and buildings make a series of strong dark shapes against the light, with a few hints of muted colour here and there. The composition is based on an elongated 'L', with the distant bank simplified and played down as it recedes further into the distance. The line of the foreshore makes an interesting shape and leads the eye into the picture. The whole work was virtually completed in two washes, with the deck detail, mooring lines and posts just suggested so as not to clutter up the image. Notice how I have allowed the washes depicting the hulls of the vessels to drift down into the water. An accent is created by the glints of light on the water, for which I used touches of masking fluid to preserve the white paper.

LEIGH BAWLEY
Watercolour,
7¼x10¼in (18x25cm)

When I first joined the Wapping Group the River Thames was still a living, working river, although even then relatively quiet compared with its heyday in the 1940s. The docks and river were littered with sailing barges, tugboats and lighters, and huge cargo ships from all over the world were anchored in the Upper and Lower Pools. The banks of the river, too, were a hive of activity, and the jumble of quays and wharves, piers and jetties, warehouses and cranes provided yet more pictorial possibilities. For me, it was all a new and exciting challenge. Thirty years on, I am proud to be President of the Wapping Group and still regularly attend the venues, although these days I have to work a little harder to seek out interesting aspects to paint. Where it runs through the City, the previously bustling Thames is now just a muted echo of its former self, and the once-booming docks are now an eerily quiet urban prairie dotted with glassy modern office blocks and executive apartments. Even so, with any watery subject the prevailing light effects can change an uninspiring scene and transform it into something magical, and Docklands is no exception. I have also noticed that there is a marked increase in river traffic a couple of hours before and after high water, as vessels take advantage of the movement of the rising and falling tide, so this is often a rewarding time to paint.

As well as being a 'Wapper' I have also been a member of the Royal Society of Marine Artists since 1971. I must confess I sometimes feel something of a fraud, as I'm a confirmed landlubber and know very little about the structure and workings of sailing

CUTTY SARK, GREENWICH
Watercolour,
13x10in (33x25cm)

vessels. (No good asking me to joggle the futtocks, fluke the mizzen or shackle the rowlocks; you would be met with a blank and uncomprehending stare.) My interest in all things floating is a purely visual one. Whether it's a rusty old tugboat or an elegant schooner, a tiny dinghy or a huge tanker, I love them all. I particularly admire the traditional hand-crafted boats, like the Leigh Bawley (a small fishing smack used for harvesting cockles from the Thames Estuary – see the painting opposite) or the Staithes Coble (a small, open, flat-bottomed boat with a high prow and stern used for fishing in the North Sea off the north-east coast of England). I also like the traditional sailing barges which are still seen now and again on the Thames, looking so majestic in full rig with their tan-coloured sails. When abroad, I love to paint the traditional fishing caiques in the Mediterranean, and the little feluccas with huge white sails that ply the waters of the Nile. Such craft are of local origin and display a beautiful line and fine proportions, developed and honed over centuries of use.

Above
FILTERED LIGHT, GWEEK
Watercolour, 10x14in (26x36cm)

The morning was still and quiet, with just the merest hint of light percolating through the low cloud cover. The large boat with the blue tarpaulin and its reflection I placed off-centre to the right, allowing the eye to wend its way over the wet mud towards the distant building with its roof picking up the light from the sky. The bank of trees to the left caused the tone of the adjacent mud to appear darker, and also picked out the line of the shallow channel meandering in front of the building. Fortunately the light remained constant throughout the whole process of painting the picture; just as I was bringing it to conclusion the sun finally burst through and transformed the whole atmosphere of the creek.

Opposite
FALMOUTH, DRY DOCK
Watercolour, 13x9½in (33x24cm)

I struck lucky with this elevated view of a big tanker in dry dock as you don't often see a dockyard scene like this in Britain today. The subject was interesting enough in itself, but what really attracted me was the light. It was late afternoon and much of the foreground was steeped in deep, dark shadow, save for one part of the tanker's hull which was dramatically spotlit by the low sun streaking across from the left. You can just make out two tiny figures working on a platform at the base of the hull, which give a good idea of the enormous scale of the vessel. I have simplified and suggested the paraphernalia on the ship's deck and the quayside to give an impression of activity without detracting from the impact of the light on the hull.

THREE SKIFFS
Watercolour,
7x10in (18x25cm)

Despite my lack of sea legs, sailing aficionados say that the ships and boats in my paintings do look convincing, so the many cold, damp hours I have spent patiently observing, sketching and painting them seem to have paid off. I try not to get bogged down in details when drawing boats, but it is essential to get their basic shapes and proportions right. Each vessel has its own character, conveyed in its individual shapes and lines: the curve of the gunwales, the rake of the bow and the angle of the transom. In order to draw them accurately I have to look repeatedly at my drawing and back at the subject, making constant critical comparisons and checking shapes and angles. The first thing is to check that the length of the boat is in proportion to the height of the mast. Then I can compare, say, the length of the cabin compared with the length of the boat, and so on.

Boats in a painting must harmonize with their surroundings. Being solid, man-made structures, it is a common mistake to overstate them with too many dark tones and hard edges, so making them appear clumsy and at odds with the surrounding elements of sky and water. Masts and rigging, for example, should not be laboured over but simplified and suggested with lost-and-found lines. *Cutty Sark, Greenwich* (page 67) is an example of this; the famous old tea clipper, berthed in dry dock in Greenwich, has a very complicated arrangement of masts and rigging and I had to half-close my eyes and then deftly sketch them in using both a dry-brush technique and a rigger.

STORM CLOUDS, RIVER ALDE
Watercolour,
5x7in (12x18cm)

Although the basic drawing is obviously important, an exact physical representation is unnecessary. Rather, I strive to capture the character of a particular boat and to suggest movement and the play of wind and light on its surfaces. Most importantly, a boat must look as if it is sitting *in* the water and not *on* it, and this is achieved by allowing some of the initial wash for the boat's hull to drift down into the water below, avoiding any hard edges at the waterline. Another thing I find fascinating is the pattern of reflected light thrown up off the water on to the hull; small touches like this lend atmosphere and luminosity to a marinescape.

When handling coastal waters you must always take into account the timing and movement of the tides. I remember once painting a harbour with fishing boats moored along the quayside on which I was standing. I started the painting at high water, and was so absorbed in my work that I failed to notice that the tide was falling; when I came to paint the boats, all I could see were the masts! Of course the reverse can happen, and your view of a low-water subject can become completely obscured as a foreground vessel rises on the tide. It is wise to try to anticipate the level of the water in, say, two to three hours' time and pitch your work so that it spans the period to include an hour or so each side of either high or low water. The water level will then remain fairly constant and you will not be faced with major changes to your subject.

OFF WAPPING
Watercolour,
7x10in (18x25cm)

BREAKERS, SOUTHWOLD
Watercolour,
$7^1/_4$x$10^1/_4$in (18x25cm)

Marine subjects certainly offer a wealth of pictorial possibilities. One might, as Turner did, choose to confront the elemental forces of nature in the wide expanses of sea, sky and beach – for which the fluid, mercurial qualities of watercolour are tailor-made. Or perhaps introduce the human element and portray those places where the land meets the sea: ports and harbours, fishing villages and seaside towns, many of which still retain a rich heritage of traditional architecture. I particularly enjoy those archetypal British seaside resorts such as Brighton and Sidmouth, with their pastel-painted stucco façades and decorative wrought-iron and plasterwork, all contributing to a timeless air that never fails to enchant the visitor.

Harbours and estuaries with their ships, docks and boatyards are a favourite theme of mine and provide a rich source of painting material: boats, piers and jetties, gantries, boat sheds, water and reflections, and of course figures or groups of figures. Rather than attempt to take in the entire view I try to find a small element that catches my eye and triggers the desire to paint, such as someone repainting a boat hull, or the way a shadow cuts across a boat and forms an interesting pattern of light and dark, or perhaps the colour of a patch of sunlit muddy water at low tide. I love the general air of fond neglect about these places and the weather-worn appearance of old boats, rotting timbers and bits of flotsam and jetsam found in the area between high and low tide.

Opposite
EVENING SHADOWS, ALDEBURGH SEAFRONT
Watercolour,
13x10in (33x25cm)

T Chamberlain

PORTHMEOR BEACH, ST IVES
Watercolour,
14x21in (36x53cm)

CLOUD SHADOWS, DEVON
Watercolour, 7x10in (18x25cm)

The dramatic shape of the limestone cliff-face is one of the main features of this cove at Beer in Devon. The sky on this particular day was sunny but with broken cloud. Cloud shadows were moving slowly across the light-coloured beach and cliff, and over the surface of the sea, creating lots of interesting patterns. In order to fully appreciate the effect they created I chose an elevated viewpoint. Having sketched in the general layout, I then had to decide which particular arrangement of shadows I wanted, bearing in mind the importance of preserving and enhancing the shape of the cliff edge itself. I indicated small groups of figures and boats to give a sense of scale. The line of beach huts on the left forms a lead-in and also gives weight and stability to the composition.

REFLECTED LIGHT, NEFYN HARBOUR
Watercolour, 7x10in (18x25cm)

This painting is very much about light, bouncing off the wet sand with almost blinding strength. When I half-closed my eyes I could discern the various tonal relationships between the boats and the background. The secondary light reflecting off the cottage roofs forms a counterbalance to the main glare of the sun on the sand. I liked the way the dinghies were resting at various angles, with their masts pointing in different directions. The reflected lights thrown up on to the boat hulls from the sand made an important contribution to the lighting effect, and there is a nice counterchange of dark boats against light sand and light buildings against dark cliffs.

BRIGHTON PROMENADE
Watercolour,
7x10in (18x25cm)

The working river frontage is constantly changing, and if you are a frequent foreshore painter like myself you never know what unusual sights or experiences will come your way. I remember one occasion when I was painting by the Thames and I spotted an object floating in the shallows by a pier. It appeared to be a corpse – I hardly dared investigate further, but eventually I plucked up courage and moved closer. To my relief it was merely the thawed-out carcase of a pig, lost overboard from a freighter.

As always, I like to paint on site at all times of the year. When working outdoors, all five senses come into play, adding a further dimension which shows through in the final painting. One enduring image I have is of painting *Storm Clouds, River Alde* (page 71) on a deserted East Coast creek on a chilly day in winter with the smell of seaweed and mud in my nostrils, the melancholy silence broken only by the clinking of the halyards against the masts in the wind, the lapping of the water, and the plaintive call of a distant curlew. A chilly recollection. In complete contrast, *Porthmeor Beach, St Ives* (page 76) was an extremely exhilarating subject. It was a bright day in high summer, but with a stiff breeze blowing off the Atlantic, and the fast-moving cumulus clouds were casting moving patterns of light and shadow over the beach and water. The subject merited a large painting, but because the wind was so strong I was only able to do a small watercolour sketch and use this, and my memory, as the basis for the finished painting back in the studio. I was keen to convey the impression of a lively day, but it was quite a task as there was so much going on. I had to work fast to nail my initial response to the scene and capture the

LIGHTERS BY 'THE ANGEL', ROTHERHITHE
Watercolour, 7x10in (18x25cm)

essentials – the moving clouds and breakers, the lovely shadows and reflections on the wet sand, the way the hill with the building on top cuts into the sky. In a changing light it is necessary to commit to a particular arrangement of clouds, shadows and so on and stick with it, working with the changing scene while retaining that initial mental image.

Near the sea, the light bounces off the water through the salt-laden moist atmosphere, evident even on a clear, bright day, giving it a unique, bewitching quality. The end of the day can be particularly atmospheric, especially when looking directly into the sun, accentuating the warm tones and simplifying form. Marine subjects are open to wide interpretation, from quiet, close-toned, moody impressions with a few well-placed accents, in the manner of Turner, to the colourful, vibrant, busy dock scenes reminiscent of the work of Sir Frank Brangwyn, RA. In a musical analogy, the former could be compared to a violin sonata and the latter to a full-blown symphony, but both would need to be conceived stressing the same fundamentals of structure, harmony, tone, colour and feeling.

On-site marine painting arguably presents more adverse conditions and throws up greater obstacles for the artist than most other branches of painting. As well as the changing light and weather, there are many other problems: the tide patterns, the movement of ships and boats, the often exposed nature of the location, the precarious positions which always seem to be the best vantage points, and often being in the way of other folk going about their tasks. Yet in spite of all the difficulties, there is plenty to stir the imagination. For me, at least, the combination of air, light and water will always be irresistible.

SPRING MORNING, BY THE RIVER BLYTH
Watercolour, 9x12½in (22x32cm)

Walberswick, by the River Blyth in Suffolk, is a well-known magnet for painters. A century ago, when it was mainly a fishing community, the village spawned an artists' colony which included among its members such renowned painters as Philip Wilson Steer and Charles Rennie Mackintosh.

Overlooking the North Sea, Walberswick can sometimes be cold, bleak, and susceptible to sea frets. However, on the day I painted this watercolour it was a delightful clear spring morning with just a hint of freshness. I was drawn to the old fisherman's hut, with its weatherbeaten, sun-bleached planking providing a perfect foil for the clean-cut white boats in the foreground, together forming an L-shaped composition. The background activity of boats and sails gives interest and animation within the angle formed by the hut and the boats.

Opposite
CANVAS AWNING, CAMPO SANTA MARGHERITA
Watercolour, 6½x9½in (16x24cm)

It isn't necessary always to paint grand vistas and important buildings. I like to seek out the commonplace, everyday elements that characterize the atmosphere of a particular city. A market stall, a quiet back street, a jumble of rooftops and chimneys – there are so many aspects to explore. On my way to paint along the Grand Canal in Venice, I was immediately seduced by this little market because of the warm light shining through the canvas awning. To focus attention on this area, I deliberately simplified and subdued the background and placed some dark tones in front of it to provide contrast. Having completed the painting, I happily continued to my original destination.

Above
SUNDAY MORNING, NORTH ROAD, HERTFORD
Watercolour, 7x10in (18x25cm)

Here is an example of how light and atmosphere can transform even an ordinary street. The trees, buildings and road are softened by the misty light, an effect which I have tried to capture using a limited range of colour and tonal values. Notice how the bottom of the building melts into the shadowy tones of the street so that they merge together with no hard lines. The bright light on the roof – an area of bare white paper – forms a strong focal point, counterbalanced by the smaller highlight further to the right. The darks in the foreground help to accentuate the mistiness in the distance. The figure and road sign on the left were very light in tone but I deliberately toned them down, otherwise they would have been out of key.

Above
STONE AND TERRACOTTA, VENICE
Watercolour, 10x14in (25x35cm)

I aim to create a good abstract pattern in my townscapes, choosing a few broad main shapes and arranging them in the picture space to form a unified design. Townscapes have a built-in advantage here, of course, as the recurring verticals, horizontals, squares and rectangles created by walls, windows and doorways are powerful compositional tools. Here, the foreground shadow is an important element in the picture as it underlines the L-shaped composition and provides a 'frame' for the main subject.

There were a lot of ornate architectural details on these façades, but I tried to simplify them while conveying something of their character. Layout and form, shapes, shadows and light; these are the first essentials.

Opposite
TATE GALLERY PORTICO
Watercolour, 14x10in (36x26cm)

One can always find something to paint in the city, even on a grey, seemingly uninspiring day. This subject was painted under difficult conditions, what with traffic thundering by and hordes of inquisitive tourists milling about. Nevertheless I enjoyed painting it; I was fascinated by the grand scale and imposing solidity of the building, juxtaposed with the colour and motion of the tiny figures on the steps. Despite the absence of strong light, there were some interesting tonal contrasts; I liked the way the portico created a deep shadow behind the light-struck columns, for instance, and the counterchange of the dark statues on the roof against a light patch of sky. The dark railings made a nice accent, but I have merely suggested them so that they don't bar the way into the picture.

Dealing with light and shadow and creating mood and atmosphere are elements of painting that must rely on personal experience. You have to feel these sensations at first hand before you can hope to express them in paint, and this means, of course, painting on location. Unfortunately it also means enduring the distractions of traffic and people. I'm the shy, retiring type and hate to be watched while I'm painting, but of course curious onlookers are even more of a hazard in the city than they are in the countryside. The minute you set up your easel in the street you are prey to the inquisitive gaze of passers-by. Even after fifty-odd years as a painter, it still takes great courage for me to paint or draw in a public place. However, once I have overcome my initial reticence and become engrossed in tackling the complexities of the subject, everything else fades into the background. To avoid onlookers breathing down my neck, where possible I will stand in a corner or with my back against a wall. And if anyone has the temerity to start chatting, I have learned the knack of grunting in the right places while keeping my concentration on the painting. Other avoidance tactics include painting the view from a hotel balcony, which affords not only privacy but also some interesting bird's-eye compositions, and working very early in the morning, before there are too many people about.

Architectural subjects can provide images that are strong and dramatic, as well as atmospheric and beautiful. Often it is not the buildings themselves that appeal, but how they are affected by light, and to this end I like to paint in the early morning or late afternoon to take full advantage of the play of shadows. In the misty sunshine of early morning, buildings and streets can have a magical quality, bathed in a delicate haze. Similarly at dusk, the shapes of buildings are simplified and the backlit silhouettes of figures and objects in the street are surrounded by brilliant haloes of light. In late afternoon, deep linking shadows are cast across the street and up the sides of buildings, creating strong, almost abstract shapes that make dramatic compositions. Sometimes the effect is almost theatrical, as when a sunlit building is glimpsed at the end of a shadowy street, or when the tops of buildings are illuminated by the setting sun and everything at street level is diffused in shadow.

I enjoy the challenge of painting in all weathers and not just on sunny days. Depending on the particular location, rainy streets might have a melancholy air or they might conjure up the vitality of city life, with colourful bright lights reflected on wet roads and pavements. Passing showers and thunderstorms bring in their wake fresh visual excitement when the sun re-emerges, often with startling contrasts of sunshine and cloud, as in *Passing Rain, Dieppe* (opposite). Snow and mist will transform even the most familiar street into something strange and other-worldly. Even on a dull, grey day when there are no shadows to speak of there will be a hint of filtered light from the sky and, if you choose your subject wisely, with its own built-in darks and lights, it is possible to create a painting with mood and atmosphere. Indeed the unchanging light can be an advantage as you don't have to cope with strong shadows that constantly move and change. *Tate Gallery Portico* (page 87) was painted on such a day and I think the subdued tones and colours somehow underline the dignity and gravitas of this venerable old gallery.

Time is a key factor when working on location. I do very little in the way of preliminary sketching and planning; generally I look at the subject through half-closed eyes, weigh it up and see how it will compose. It may be necessary to adjust what I see, to play something up or down, but the important thing is to try to nail my initial response as quickly as possible. I work with furious concentration and aim to finish a painting in a maximum of three hours, usually much less, always aware of the changing light and

Opposite
PASSING RAIN, DIEPPE
Watercolour, 21x17in (53x43cm)

T. Chamberlain '86

T. Chamberlain

SHIV NIWAS PALACE, UDAIPUR
Watercolour,
10x14in (25x35cm)

shadows. In transient conditions I will map in the shadows in the early stages and ignore any subsequent changes.

When tackling architecture, and particularly classical architecture, the drawing element assumes far greater significance. It is particularly important to get the proportions right, to compare the height of the building in relation to its width and to get the scale of doors and windows right in relation to the building. The characteristic features and embellishments of the building need to be carefully observed, but not overstated; they should be seen through half-closed eyes and then suggested in broad terms; banks of windows, for example, should be suggested simply and some missed out altogether. Try to relate the details to the underlying structure from the start, rather than tagging them on at the end. Some buildings can overwhelm with their detail, but a painting that shows every brick and glazing bar will lack vigour and appear awkward and laboured: it leaves nothing to the imagination of the viewer. Often, the suggestion of texture, pattern or detail is all that's needed to convey the whole story; the viewer actually gets more out of the picture when he or she is required to 'fill in' the details from imagination. Experience develops a kind of painter's shorthand that suggests rather than copies the details of buildings. At the same time, beware of adopting facile and gimmicky habits; there is a fine line between the assured brevity that comes from dedicated practice and observation and the meretricious and easy effects of the lazy painter. It's like the difference between

BUILDING WORKS, BRIGHTON PAVILION
Watercolour,
10 1/2 x 14 3/4in (26x37cm)

the dramatic and the theatrical: the former has integrity, the latter is shallow and showy.

In common with the way I tackle other subjects, I aim for a controlled looseness of colour in my townscapes. I start with an overall wet wash with the passages of darker colour dropped into it and preserving any light areas. Because of the way buildings face each other, reflected lights are often in abundance and leafy trees cast dappled patterns of light and shadow across roads and façades. It is therefore necessary to allow for chinks of light in my first wash. With my second application I do some drawing with the brush, making crisp edges in the sunlight and blurring forms and softening edges in the shadows. One can observe, for instance, how direct sunlight picks out the contours of any projections and mouldings, while those in shadow are more muted and should merely be hinted at. All the while I try to retain the breadth of execution while keeping the initial idea alive, the reason for painting the picture in the first place: the contrast and shape of a shadow falling across a street, a group of men working under an awning, or simply some striking effect of light.

Architectural details, both decorative and functional, can be just as interesting as the buildings themselves, and a single arch, doorway, balcony or window can make a satisfying study in its own right. Likewise, fountains, monuments and figurative sculpture can be fascinating if demanding subjects requiring accurate drawing and an awareness of textures and reflected lights, though once again one must beware of overworking. John Singer Sargent was a master at painting such subjects in watercolour, and his paintings are worthy of study in this respect.

Streets and buildings are centres of human activity, and in many of my paintings it is the relationship between figures and their environment that provides the main interest. I am always fascinated by the contrast between the fixed solidity of buildings and the ceaseless activity of people and cars in the street below. I will talk in more detail about painting incidental figures in chapter six, but suffice to say here that they should never be overstated or hard-edged. The lighting conditions may cause parts of the figure to appear to blend into the background, and much of the poetry of a painting is attained by softening an edge here and losing a detail there, so as to convey movement and integrate the figure into its surroundings. Where there are several figures scattered about in a street, select just some of them and group them in an interesting way with perhaps an individual picked out here and there. When I painted *Tate Gallery Portico* (page 87) there was a crowd milling about on the steps, so I selected certain elements only and arranged them into interesting groups with a few individuals here and there. The lost-and-found quality of the figures acknowledges that the people are just a fleeting incident compared with the permanence of the great building.

Cars and other vehicles, though often lacking in picturesque qualities, are an inevitable feature of modern life and should be included in street scenes to add realism. Vehicles are often brash, shiny, brightly coloured objects with boxy shapes and need to be sensitively handled and treated as incidentals in the picture. As with figures, suggestion is the key: as long as the silhouette and proportions are right it's surprising how little detail you can get away with. You don't have to paint every car that's there; just one or two are enough to suggest the bustle and activity of a busy street, and they can always be positioned in the distance or middle distance rather than the foreground.

Over the years I have painted in countless towns and cities, both at home and abroad. There are so many fascinating architectural styles, and every place has its own flavour, but I think my favourite city is Venice. On my first visit in 1966 I fell in love with its magical

Above
RAIN, PRAGUE
Watercolour,
5x7in (12x18cm)

combination of architecture, nature and people, all enveloped in the shimmering light that reflects off the canal and gives luminosity. There is a feeling of stepping back in time to a more elegant age, partly because there are no cars and also because everywhere there is an atmosphere of pleasing decay; I love the faded grandeur of the baroque and Italianate buildings with their crumbling stucco façades gently decaying at the waterline, and the varied shapes of windows and doors, often irregularly positioned rather than in regimented rows.

Of course, Venice is so well known and so often painted, and one is humbly aware of following in the footsteps of the likes of Turner, Sargent and Brabazon, not to mention contemporary painters such as Ken Howard and Bernard Dunstan. But Venice really is an artist's dream. Every new turn provides dazzling architecture, bridges, canals and squares with trees and statues, and there is also the hidden Venice, the quiet canals and humble little churches and houses away from the tourist areas. There is always something new to say, especially in view of the magical effects of light in different seasons and at different times of the day. I particularly like dusk in Venice, when there is a wonderful combination of soft, dark shapes and luminous sky, accented by the sharp electric lights of windows

Opposite
THE BLUE HOUSE, UDAIPUR
Watercolour,
10x7in (25x18cm)

TWILIGHT, VENICE LAGOON
Watercolour,
20x28in (50x71cm)

A QUIET CANAL IN VENICE
Watercolour, 7x10in (18x25cm)

When visiting Venice I like to slip away to the quiet back streets and small canals away from the throngs of tourists and savour the tranquil sounds of distant bells ringing, gondoliers calling, the gentle lapping of water and the echoing pad of footsteps. And to paint delightful scenes such as this, which to my mind capture the essence of the city as well as any grand vista of the Grand Canal.

Watercolour is, of course, the ideal medium for recording Venice's watery charms. In this picture the boats and buildings are reflected in the murky, still water of the canal and the buildings cast shadows across the surface, creating pleasing shapes of light and dark. There is an overall feeling of warmth, which is helped by the mellow tone of the tinted paper.

SPARKLING MORNING, THE ZATTERE, VENICE
Watercolour, 10x14in (25x35cm)

and street lamps. *Twilight, Venice Lagoon* (page 97) captures my memory of just such an evening. I was on a painting trip to Venice with fellow-artist David Curtis and during an evening stroll before dinner we decided to take in the view from the top of the Campanile tower in St Mark's Square. And what a view it was, absolutely breathtaking. In the milky twilight the church of Santa Maria della Salute in the foreground, and the smaller islands in the distance, made ethereal dark shapes on the lagoon, with just a few points of light here and there. We didn't have so much as a sketchbook between us, let alone paints and brushes (frustrating, not to say pretty foolish, for two such experienced artists wandering around the world's most beautiful city!), so we had to make do with taking photographs. Nevertheless, the image was so unforgettable that, back in England, I was able to rekindle the experience to finish the painting mostly from memory, using the photographs as reference.

The Czech capital of Prague is another architectural jewel. The city emerged from the Second World War relatively unscathed and so escaped the heavy hand of redevelopment during the Cold War period, but it is only in recent years that its beauty has been rediscovered. Prague is positively littered with castles, churches and cathedrals, and the architecture is astonishingly varied: Gothic, Romanesque, baroque and rococo buildings abound, and the wealth of art-nouveau decoration is particularly memorable. Almost

Opposite
BAROQUE CHURCH DOORWAY, PRAGUE
Watercolour, 14x10in (35x25cm)

STREET IN PAWCATUCK, CONNECTICUT
Watercolour, 10x14in (25x35cm)

Vehicles, like people, have an annoying habit of moving about and disappearing before we have a chance to paint them. Thumbnail sketches can help, but if you can cultivate a good visual memory it will enable you to deal with this problem more effectively. While I was painting this street scene I spotted a shiny red American truck in the distance and I knew I just had to get it in to the picture. It was approaching at some speed, and I only had time to sketch a rough impression of it before it roared past me in a whirl of dust and exhaust smoke. I tried to log in my mind the positions of the tones and colours on the truck and painted it from memory. It is just convincing enough to read as a truck, but you don't need any more than that, really; suggestion is the key.

Opposite
WALTHAM ABBEY
Watercolour,
10x7in (25x18cm)

every building is encrusted inside and out with fine, elaborate, sometimes witty designs in stone, plaster, wood, wrought-iron, stained glass and mosaic. With such a wealth of detail I find it useful to make preliminary sketches before painting, and to go for the general character of the street or building rather than trying to pin down everything I see.

Baroque Church Doorway, Prague (page 100) was painted on a recent visit to the city with Bert Wright, a painter friend. We spotted this attractive doorway in the old town square on our way back to our hotel for breakfast after an early morning painting session. We didn't have time to paint it there and then, but resolved to return the next morning, hoping that the lighting conditions would be the same. Luckily it stayed sunny long enough for us to get the wonderful shadows and reflected lights down on to our sheets, and photographs gave us enough back-up information to complete our paintings back home. It was an intense, concentrated period of working in a deteriorating light but I often feel that when you are fired up and working under pressure it concentrates the mind on the essentials and introduces a sense of urgency into your painting.

Painting abroad is always a thrilling experience but it does pose climatic problems for the watercolourist. In some parts of the world it is often so hot that washes dry almost before you have laid them on the paper. I remember once when painting in Iran, I sponged the sheet three times before starting to paint and still the paper was dry before I had finished the first wash. Conversely, in humid climates such as I experienced in South Carolina recently, the washes refuse to dry at all! Something else to contend with is the different quality of the light abroad. It takes a while to get used to the clarity of the light and the saturated colours in hot, dry climates after the soft grey light of Britain.

My love of mist, haze and smoke makes painting in desert regions very enjoyable for me. In Egypt, for instance, the air bears fine particles of sand so that the light is filtered through a warm gossamer veil which, combined with the light-toned colour-washed buildings, gives a feeling of airiness to the whole atmosphere, with even the shadow areas full of light reflecting back off surrounding surfaces. In India there are two-stroke motorized rickshaws everywhere, belching out their choking fumes. Whole streets disappear into a blue haze which, when backlit by the sun, creates a magical effect (I have tried to capture it in *Traffic Haze, Udaipur,* page 105). Through the fumes lots of colour is still discernible, ranging from the locals' dress to bazaar awnings and market stalls piled high with exotic fruits and spices of every hue. All of this is wonderful painting material, but the heat and the smells and the noise which assail you from every side can make it difficult to concentrate on the job in hand. If after all this you still decide to set up an easel in the street, within a few moments you will be surrounded by a swarm of peering, pushing, poking children who view you with enormous curiosity, quite as much fascinated by you as you are with them and their locality. Even a seemingly quiet corner of the countryside becomes the busiest place in the district as soon as you set up; people just seem to spring out of the earth. The only way to work unhindered is to hire a local to keep the crowds at bay. Sometimes, of course, the shoe is on the other foot and you are the nuisance. When I was painting *Light and Shade, Shiraz Bazaar* (page 22) in Iran a local man took great exception to me painting the mosque and the people in the market in front of it and became quite aggressive. Luckily I had an Armenian friend with me who managed to fend him off, otherwise I might have become the victim of a fatwah! This story illustrates how important it is to remember that, when abroad, you are the foreigner. Always be sensitive to and have respect for the local culture and traditions whenever you set out to paint.

Above
MAUSOLEUM, ASWAN
Watercolour, 7x10in (18x25cm)

Rarely does such a quiet, simple but strong image present itself, requiring no re-arranging or 'artistic licence'. Seen in that first tremulous heat of the day, it had everything I could wish for - atmosphere, light, composition, colour harmony, tonal balance, texture and an interesting sky-line. I used an old Whatman rough paper which proved to be ideally suited to the textures of the stone building set in an arid rocky landscape, resulting (I hope) in a poetic, harmonious work which recalled that shimmering early light bouncing off the various surfaces. The tree group in the middle distance provided a perfect foil for the sunlit façade.

Opposite
TRAFFIC HAZE, UDAIPUR
Watercolour, 14x11in (35x28cm)

In contrast to the painting above, this subject was a full-blown symphony of colour, activity and architectural detail, which receded into the distance bathed in the blue exhaust fumes from the motorized rickshaws and scooters. Choosing an old cream-tinted Whatman paper it was obvious that I had to simplify extensively, hinting at detail and decoration in an impressionistic manner. I positioned and grouped figures, treating them as colourful stepping-stones leading the onlooker through the picture, with an accent provided by just one woman caught in a shaft of light.

In Eastern countries it is wonderful to see so many people wearing traditional dress, giving a timeless feel to the scene. Unfortunately, the T-shirt, jeans, trainers and baseball cap are making their insidious presence felt, universally spoiling the character of individual places.

Chapter Six

FIGURES

Most of my paintings of landscapes and townscapes include figures because I find that an element of active involvement in a scene helps to bring it to life. Figures and animals introduce movement, colour and character to a scene, and provide a useful scale by which we recognize relative heights and distances. Understandably, less-experienced artists are often intimidated by the prospect of painting figures and animals – especially moving ones – and banish them from their landscapes and street scenes altogether, thus lending them a perpetual 'Sunday morning' atmosphere. On the other hand, I have also seen many a good picture ruined by the inclusion of figures that are wooden and lacking in life or movement, are too hard in tone and colour, and with heads that are too big!

Unless you intend painting nothing but still lifes, I consider it essential for you to learn how to draw and paint the human figure. This doesn't require a surgeon's knowledge of anatomy, but you will need to spend time observing, sketching and painting people in a variety of situations. Draw your family and friends, find places where people congregate – cafés, markets, train stations – and fill lots of sketchbooks with quick studies. I cannot stress enough the importance of developing your drawing and observational skills. Only by doing so will you gain an intuitive feel for the proportions and rhythms inherent in the human form. This instinctive response is vital when you are working *in situ*, where

CASTING METAL
Watercolour, 7x10in (18x25cm)

ENTRANCE TO PALAZZO PUBBLICO, SIENA
Watercolour, 10x7in (25x18cm)

the pressures of time demand the ability to whip a figure into place with both speed and brevity.

Of course, people in the street are not going to stop what they're doing and pose for you; indeed, they will probably have wandered off-stage before you can get brush to paper. But remember, you are not painting portraits; there is no need to concern yourself with details such as facial features and hands. After all, you don't need to see someone's features to recognize them from a distance; they can usually be identified simply by their bulk, stance and gait. The main aim when painting incidental figures is to suggest movement, light and scale. So long as you get the basic proportions right and describe their movements and gestures, it is possible to suggest incidental figures with just a few brush strokes. In *Entrance to Palazzo Pubblico, Siena* (above), for example, the figures are glimpsed in the distance and I have suggested them with just a few smudgy marks and dots, yet they 'read' as human figures because the eye and imagination fill in the details. I have not painted the hands, for instance, and the legs appear to fade out towards the ground because the figures are moving and because the lower legs are partially dissolved by light reflecting upwards.

Above
SKETCHES OF BRUSSELS SPROUT PICKERS
Pencil, 6½x5in (16x12cm)

Left
BRUSSELS SPROUT PICKING, BEDFORDSHIRE
Watercolour, 10¼x14¼in (25x35cm)

My painting colleagues often joke that I am tucked away in an unlikely spot, far away from the obvious picturesque scene: 'Oh, Trevor's over there, behind the pigsty painting a bonfire. . .' But I find that often, the most rewarding paintings can be of simple, everyday scenes and activities.

There is a kind of 'humble grandeur' about this sort of scene which always strikes a chord in me. The figures were moving all the time, so I decided where I wanted to position them in the composition and allowed for them when painting the landscape. I then made sketches of the figures (see above) and used them as reference when completing the painting back in the studio.

Before attempting to paint the figure, practise making free, gestural drawings using a variety of media such as charcoal, chalk, pencil, graphite stick, brush and ink or felt-tipped pen. Give yourself a time-limit of, say, ten minutes (as I did in the figure sketches here) and try to capture the essence of the pose as simply as possible, avoiding superfluous marks that contribute nothing to the main idea.

LAZY DAY, SUMMER 1989
Watercolour, 9x13in (22x33cm)

I was immediately struck by the pictorial possibilities of this family group lounging under the trees on a very hot summer day. They were all reading and dozing and it was obvious they weren't going to go very far, so I seized the opportunity to paint them. I tucked myself away in the shade to avoid the problems of glare on the paper and the washes drying too quickly.

I like the repeated arrangement of the deckchairs and figures, which sets up a nice rhythm across the paper. The central figures are steeped in dappled shade so they are worked wet-into-wet to create a play of lost-and-found edges. The lit figure in the background is more crisply stated; it strikes a nice contrasting note with the figures in shade. I have simplified the background in order to focus attention on to the group of figures.

CROQUET ON THE SEA-FRONT AT SIDMOUTH
Watercolour,
7x10in (18x25cm)

Sometimes you may wish to treat a figure or a group more prominently in the picture, in which case they must be more carefully observed and stated – although even here, simplicity is the key. When making a feature of figures I tend to choose people engaged in some repetitive or sedentary activity like sunbathing, reading, fishing or playing a sport or a musical instrument. As a precaution against them suddenly moving away or getting rained off, I might make a quick drawing or even take a snapshot for reference. (I would not advise copying from photographs because they tend to flatten forms and freeze movement; however, they can be a useful *aide-mémoire.*)

When a human figure is included in a composition, the eye is inevitably drawn to it, even if it is little more than a tiny dot in the distance. For this reason, a well-placed figure or group of figures can either form the focal point of a composition or provide a pointer to it by leading the viewer's eye in the direction in which they are moving or looking. In *Tram Terminus, Fleetwood Promenade* (page 32), for example, the strong counterchange of the line of dark figures against a light background attracts the eye and leads us into the picture from left to right.

In watercolour it is important to decide at the outset where you want to position the figures within the composition and then allow for them when applying the initial background wash. This way, the figures will integrate naturally with their surroundings rather than looking as though they have been pasted on as an afterthought. When

STILL-LIFE SESSION
AT THE SEED WAREHOUSE
Watercolour,
10x14in (25x35cm)

painting *Lazy Day, Summer 1989* (page 112) I indicated the figures by making some random, varied marks into my initial wash, leaving tiny chinks of white for the brightest highlights on the background figure's hat and shoulder. By making these random marks initially I produced a free statement, one that did not influence too strongly my subsequent painting of the figures. (The alternative – drawing an outline of the figure and filling it in with colour – only encourages that wooden, cut-out effect since the figure is at once divorced from its surroundings.) When the initial wash was dry I worked a little more refinement into the figures, developing the existing marks to suggest form, movement, light and shadow. It is important not to *over*work, of course, but to retain an impressionistic effect so that the figures harmonize with the rest of the picture.

Paintings in which a portrait, clothed figure or nude form the main subject are quite a challenge, especially in watercolour. Unlike oil painting, you have to get it right first time because if you re-work a passage you risk losing the freshness and luminosity in the skin tones. Another difficulty is that because so many great artists of the past have painted the nude, it can be difficult to disassociate from their work and come up with a fresh, imaginative approach to the subject. Nevertheless, even a small measure of experience will reveal exciting possibilities for new ideas; the main thing is to be inspired by what you see and to discover your own voice in interpreting it effectively. I still regularly attend life classes at my local art society, and I never tire of the subject because there is always

NUBIAN MOTHER AND DAUGHTER
Watercolour,
$7^1/_2$x6in (19x15cm)

something new to learn. There is a danger of going into 'auto-pilot' mode when painting the landscape, but drawing the figure really keeps you on your toes because you have to observe the physical characteristics of the body carefully and objectively, while at the same time capturing the individuality of the person. I cannot stress enough the importance of work and practice in this field.

Life drawing develops powers of observation, a keen and analytical eye, and provides a store of essential knowledge about the postures and attitudes of the human body, all of which can be used almost unconsciously in your wider work. As an illustration of the value and importance of brevity, there is a nice little story about the great Russian film director, Sergei Eisenstein, who was selling a drawing to a client. The drawing was a visual for one of his film sets, and consisted of just a few lines. When the client complained at the price he was charging, Eisenstein replied tartly, 'If I could have done it with half as many lines, I would have charged twice as much'.

Whether drawing the nude or the clothed figure, the basic strategy must be the same. The figure must be seen in terms of simple forms that fit together. Try to understand how

the weight is distributed, the proportions and bulk of the body, the way the light picks out the shapes with lost-and-found edges, passages in shadow, and areas of reflected light within the shadows. Some elementary grasp of anatomy is useful, although careful observation will reveal important aspects of this. Hands can be surprisingly difficult, and the skill of a good figure or portrait painter is evidenced by the quality of the hands. A tip to bear in mind when you are constructing the figure on paper is to look for the negative shapes, ie the shapes made by the body in relation to itself and also to other adjacent objects.

When it comes to painting portraits and figures, one of the most common failures I come across is that of first painting the figure to a high degree of finish and only afterwards putting in the background. The problem here is that the figure is being painted against the bright whiteness of the paper, and when the backdrop is added it completely upsets the figure's tonal and colour balance. It is important to look at both subject and background as one, and not to treat them separately but work back and forth from one to the other as the work progresses. In so doing, figure and background will balance and complement each other to create a sense of movement and atmosphere and eliminate any feeling of woodenness.

After dampening the paper I normally begin by applying a light colour wash on to the

Opposite
RECLINING FIGURE
Watercolour, 10x14in (25x35cm)

Skin tones and tints vary enormously from person to person. Recently I painted a model who was obviously a naturist as her skin was a ruddy burnt colour all over; in complete contrast was another model whose skin was so delicately pale that it was almost translucent. I found the colour of the former more difficult to tackle to bring about a convincing result, while the latter I found much more subtle, displaying some fascinating nuances of reflected light and colour in the pearly tones and cool shadows. This painting is an example of the 'lost-and-found' handling of the figure; the upper edge of the hip and shoulder are crisply defined while the head is somewhat nebulous with its soft edges.

Above
SLEEPING NUDE
Watercolour, 15x20in (38x51cm)

Delicate, transparent and fluid, watercolour is the ideal medium for painting the human form, but it takes a lot of practice to be able to achieve the right degree of paint consistency. Too dry and the figure appears stiff and wooden; too wet and the paint runs out of control. Having drawn the model I note where the highlights are and leave them as bare paper. I don't often use masking fluid, but I have used it in this instance to preserve the sliver of bright light along the top of the model's right leg and arm. The skin tones are painted mostly wet-into-wet (or, to be more accurate, damp-into-damp, in a controlled and considered way) with just one or two crisp accents added at the dry stage. Shapes and volume are modelled with warm and cool colours.

BEFORE BALLET CLASS
Watercolour,
7x10in (18x25cm)

background. Then, preserving the highlights, I float in a warm, mid-toned colour over most of the figure; this will usually consist of a dilute wash of raw sienna and a touch of burnt sienna, to which might I add a touch of cobalt blue for the cooler skin tones. In order to retain luminosity of colour it is important to hit exactly the right tone first time, so it is worth testing a wash on scrap paper before committing it to the painting if you are not sure of it. While the initial wash is still damp I go on to develop the subtle nuances of light and colour in the flesh, looking for the cool shadows and warmer reflected lights, sometimes introducing a hint of viridian or permanent magenta. I work wet-into-wet all the time in order to retain the impression of softly rounded form, but it is done in a controlled way, with both paper and brush damp rather than dripping wet.

Before the paper starts to dry, I lift out a few soft highlights here and there. Then I might briefly indicate the foreground, all the while treating the figure and its surroundings as one. Then, when the paper starts to dry, there is a stage when I can do no more and I must leave it to dry completely, otherwise I find I am picking up the semi-dry colour and things start to go muddy.

Finally, I remove any masking fluid I have applied and go on to develop the overall tonal balance of the picture and introduce accents of colour and crisp cast shadows, aiming to add no more than one additional wash over the initial one. In order to preserve

GRANDAD
Watercolour,
13x10in (33x25cm)

the soft, lost-and-found edges, I first dampen the areas to be overpainted so that the new washes blend in softly. This has to be done with great care, otherwise things can go haywire; the trick is to just dampen rather than flood the surface, and to work with a featherlight touch. The surface is now very vulnerable again because you can easily stir up the underlying colour when adding a subsequent wash, so your next statement has to be made with a deft, sure touch. If it is too wet the wash mixes with the underlying colour, resulting in muddiness, and it fans out and dries with a hard edge or 'bloom'. I usually flick my brush across a rag so that it is just damp; that way, the dampness of the paper draws the paint out of the brush and it spreads and diffuses softly rather than gushing about unchecked.

Looking back to my early days, as a painter I realize how seldom I featured figures in my pictures, often making just a token representation – and how they suffered as a result. Over the intervening years, I have attached steadily greater importance to including a figurative element in my work. Painting the human figure is likely to make the most demands on the artist, but it also offers some of the greatest rewards.

Chapter Seven

INDOOR SUBJECTS

Opposite
SUNBURST, THE GREAT TEMPLE AT ABU SIMBEL
Watercolour, 10x7in (25x18cm)

Below
ESSEX BOAT SHED
Watercolour, 10x14in (25x35cm)

For such a dedicated outdoor painter, it may seem surprising that I should be interested in painting indoor subjects. Apart from striving to be a well-rounded artist, the inspirational impetus is, as ever, light and atmosphere. The straightforward domestic environment doesn't concern me greatly, however. I prefer the more unusual effects experienced in the workplace. Sometimes a dark, shadowy interior throws up the striking effect of a powerful light source spilling through a single, intense area such as a window or door, or within the room itself. This can create dramatic contrasts of tone and colour, as in *Sunburst, the Great Temple at Abu Simbel* (opposite). I set up my easel inside the temple at dawn so that I could capture the effect of the golden sunlight flooding in through the doorway, picking out the contours of the huge statues and bouncing off the walls and ceiling. There might also be figures working half-seen in the shadows, often

engaged in some activity which produces smoke or steam, for instance a blacksmith or a boat-builder power-sanding the hull of a vessel. I am particularly intrigued by the *contre-jour* effect of figures and objects positioned in front of a window so that they take on a mysterious, shadowy aspect, their contours lit up by a bright halo of light. This effect can be seen on the figure in *In the Studio, Tite Street* (page 125).

I have painted in boat repair yards, factories, railway stations, bus garages, shops and markets, and a few years ago I spent three days painting in a metal foundry. I have been interested in this sort of subject ever since I was a schoolboy, when my class was taken to various worksites as part of our careers guidance. One of the places we visited was Hertford gas works, where we watched the process of extracting gas from coal. Boys being boys, we were fascinated by the place and all the smoke, heat and flames. The drama of the image made quite an impression on me and years later, when I met someone whose parents owned a metal foundry, I wangled an invite and they kindly allowed me to go along and do some paintings. In the three days I was there I did two oils, four water-colours and many drawings and sketches. It was a very rewarding experience and satisfied my lust for this type of subject, which of course is all about light and smoky, steamy or dusty atmospheres. One of the paintings, *Slagging the Metal*, is shown above.

Painting indoors presents a different, if more controlled, environment from that out of

Opposite
SLAGGING THE METAL
Watercolour, 7x10in (18x25cm)

A metal foundry is not the easiest of places to set up an easel and paint, but I was so intrigued by this subject that I forgot about the heat, the noise and the bad light. I managed to do a small watercolour sketch and painted this version in the studio. The strong chiaroscuro of the subject was probably better suited to oils, but I felt I had to use watercolours in order to get it down quickly.

The picture shows a metal-worker skimming off the impurities, called 'slag', that rise to the surface when metal is melted down at high heat. It was like a scene from Dante's Inferno, with the somewhat menacing figure, clad in apron, mask and huge gloves, emerging from the darkness and dramatically lit from in front by the bubbling cauldron.

Above
DONCASTER FISH MARKET
Watercolour, 10x14in (25x37cm)

It was raining outside, so I decided to set up my easel in a corner of this busy indoor market. I was fascinated by the interplay of different kinds of light in the interior, reflecting off the various surfaces and enveloping the figures. On the left, warm light from a bank of spotlights floods down on to the stalls of fish and bounces back up on to the browsing figures, dissolving their features. In the background, figures are silhouetted against the contrastingly cool light coming in through the windows and door. Notice how the legs of the figures 'disappear' into the light reflecting up from the floor. With so much activity going on, I had to quickly decide which components to include and where to place them in the composition, and then finish off the painting in the studio the following day.

Opposite
IN THE STUDIO, TITE STREET
Watercolour,
14x10in (35x25cm)

doors. An interior subject may be naturally lit through a window or door, artificially lit from single or multiple sources and directions, or a combination of both, with sometimes dramatic or unusual results. The play of warm lights against cool, and pools of light against shadows and soft silhouettes, creates mysterious passages that are a constant source of intrigue. In *Doncaster Fish Market* (page 123) I was interested in the visual effect of the cool light from outside contrasting with the subtle, warmer artificial light of the indoor market. I had to squeeze myself into a corner and try and ignore the noise and bustle all around me, but it was a marvellous subject, full of soft edges and lost detail and with a beautiful symphony of close-toned colour.

An interior can resemble an enormous still life, and it is necessary to select, simplify and play down detail in order to create a cohesive picture. In the painting *In The Studio, Tite Street*, for example, there was a lot of painting equipment cluttering the windowsill behind the artist, but I simplified it to a few silhouetted shapes so as not to distract from the figure, and also to give the effect of shapes and objects dissolved in the bright light flooding in the window through the slightly dusty air of the studio.

Figures feature strongly in my interiors and I am fascinated particularly by the places where people work. There is always plenty of opportunity in these situations for portraying people engaged in various tasks, unconsciously acting as models. I can call on my experience in life studies to back up my depictions of figures, particularly when painting moving figures going about their business in public places or the workplace. They usually emerge and just as quickly disappear before I have a chance to note more than their scale or broad appearance. Providing I have made some sort of on-site statement in simple terms, I can then resolve them back at the studio, properly relating them within the composition, preserving the sharply lit contours and reflected lights and softening any unwanted hard edges.

Although I enjoy painting interior scenes, for some reason I rarely paint still lifes or flowers. Perhaps it's because I prefer to tackle subjects that move and change, giving a feeling of life 'on the wing'. My wife, Elaine, loves flowers and often brings them into the house, but most of the time I don't even notice them. Just occasionally, though, if the light is falling on a vase of flowers in an interesting way, my interest is awakened and I will paint

THE RELUCTANT MODEL
Watercolour,
5x6in (12x15cm)

NASTURTIUMS AND LILIES
Watercolour,
13x9¾in (33x24cm)

them there and then. In *Two Roses* (page 127), for example, I was drawn by the utter simplicity of just a couple of blooms in a plain glass vase. The subject was mainly backlit and the colours were restrained and harmonious. I also liked the way the water slightly distorted the stalks and acted like a lens reflecting a pool of light to the bottom of the vase.

The most interesting aspect of flowers is the way they interact with light. The shadows they cast on other blooms in the arrangement, and the subtle hints of reflected light in those shadows, create wonderfully subtle tones and colours. Not only do flowers reflect light, they can also admit it through their translucent petals; look at a vase of flowers on a windowsill with the light coming from behind them, making their colours glow as if lit from within. It is interesting to note that when light-coloured flowers are set against a dark background their light hues are enhanced, but when those same blooms are seen against a bright background, they become almost silhouetted and appear surprisingly dark in tone apart from any highlights or lit edges.

The characteristics of the flowers should be appreciated, whether they are exquisite orchids or simple daisies. Having decided on my composition, I observe the arrangement as a whole through half-closed eyes and try to see them as a three-dimensional group, well balanced in the vase with an interesting outline.

TWO ROSES
Watercolour, 6x8in (15x20cm)

They should not form a solid mass; there should be spaces between the blooms so that you feel you could go right through and come out the other side. Then I begin painting, relating the flowers to their surroundings and allowing for painting the vase, table and background in the initial wash. I simplify and play down the blooms as they recede around the edges of the group and give a little more emphasis and clarity to those at the front. This use of lost-and-found passages gives the idea of the flowers being living things, and also gives the group as a whole three-dimensionality. In the case of blooms that are very light-toned, intensely coloured or with sharp, clear-cut shapes, I usually work around their outlines, leaving them as untouched white paper. When the surrounding wash is dry I paint the flowers, noting the subtle changes of colour and tone as broadly as possible without losing sight of the character of the blooms, and softening edges here and there. I try not to paint flowers with more than one or two washes, letting the white paper shining through the colours emphasize the the delicate quality of the petals.

In his day, Turner produced many interior sketches in watercolour, painted in his inimitable loose, fluid manner and portraying light and richness of colour, which I find most stimulating. And whether I'm painting a vase of flowers or a man repairing a boat, light will always feature prominently.

INDEX

Italics refer to illustrations

Animals *49*, 56-7, 107, *124*
Architecture 14, 18, 84, 92, 93-5
  see also Buildings
Asymmetry 62
Atmosphere 20, 43, 84, 88
Autumn scenes *27*, 48, *59*
Ayling, George 14

Balance 62
Becker, Harry 20
Boats *21*, *30*, *37*, 41, *41*, 66, *66-70*, 67, 68, 70-1, *79*, *81*, *83*, 120
Body colour 23
Bonnard, Pierre 38
Brabazon, Hercules 36, 95
Brangwyn, Sir Frank 81
Brighton 74, *80*, *92*
Brown, Edward Archibald 16-18, 17, *17*
Brushes 32-4
Budleigh Salterton, Devon 43, *44-5*
Buildings 24, *24-9*, *31*, *46*, *51*, *58*, *61*, 84, *86-7*, 88, *89-92*, 92-3, *94-8*, 95, 99, *100-1*, 102, *103-5*, *107*

Canals *98*
Carolus-Duran, Charles Auguste Emile 20
Chaplin, Charlie 20
Climate, extreme 102
Clouds *30*, *44*, 48, 50, 54, *71*, *78*
Coastal scenes *19*, *44*, *45*, 54, *61*, 71, *74*, *75*, *76-7*, 78, 80, *80*
Colours:
  black 35
  distant 63
  mixing 34-5
  palette 34-5
  relationships 63
Composition 59-62
Constable, John 17, 20
Contre-jour effect 122
Cotman, John Sell 20
Cozens, John Robert 18
Curtis, David 35, 47, 99

Demi-teinte générale 20
Deserts 102
Design 20
Details 26, 59, 84, 92-3, 107, 124
Drawing *17*, 71, 92, 114
  brush 93
Dry-brush technique 54, 70
Dunstan, Bernard 95

Easels 36
Edges 23, 58
lost-and-found 58-9, 70, 93, 116, 119, 127
Egypt *2*, *37*, 40-2, *40-2*, 43, *53*, *104*, *121*
Eisenstein, Sergei 115
Equipment 27, 32-6
Erasers 27
Estuary scenes 64, 74, *83*
Eye level 23

Figures *35*, 51, *51*, 93, 106-19, *106-19*
  backgrounds 116-19
  hands 116
  in indoor scenes *106*, 120-2, *120*, *122-3*, 124, *125*
  in landscapes and townscapes 93, *105*, 106, 107, *107-9*, 113
  as main subject *34*, 114-16, *114-19*
  movement 106, *106*, 124
  nude 114, *116*, 117
  positioning 113-14
  sketches *109-11*
  skin tones 117, 118
Flowers 124-7, *126-7*
Fog *10*, 15, *15*, 62
Foreign countries, painting in 102
Fountains 93

Gardens *5*
Goodwin, Albert 36

Harbour scenes 64, 74, *79*
Haze *40*, *45*, 48-50, 63, 102
Highlights 23, 48, 118
Hilder, Rowland 16
Horizon 48-50
Howard, Ken 95

Impressionists 6
India *28-9*, *90-1*, *94*, 102, *105*
Indoor subjects 120-7, *120-7*
Iran *8*, 22

Knight, Charles 16

Landscapes 38-63, *49*, *56-7*
  demi-teinte générale 20
  figures in 106, *108-9*
  industrial 18
Life classes 114-15
Lifting out 26-7, 118
Light 20, 42, 81, 93
  effects of 14, 63, 66, 84, 88, 126
  indoors 124
  reflected 58, 71, 79, 93, 102, 107, 126
  source and direction 23, 46, 48, 54
Lines 62
Lutyens, Eadred 14

Marine subjects 18, 64-83
Markets *2*, *22*, *84*, *123*
Masking fluid 23, 118
Merriott, Jack 14-16, *17*, *22*
Miles, Bernard 60
Mirror, viewing painting through 27
Mists 38, *39*, 42, 46, *85*
Monet, Claude 43
Monuments 93
Mood 48
Movement 55, 93

Nature, impressions of 8, 9
Negative shapes 116
Nudes 114, *116*

Oils 10, 14, 18, 19
Onlookers 40, 88, 102

Paintboxes 35-6
Paints 34-5
Palette 34-5
Papers 27-8, 30, 32
  stretching 32
Pasmore, Victor 14
Perspective 48, 62-3
Photographs 99, 113
Pissarro, Camille 6
Planning 10
Plein air (outdoor) painting 6, 20, 38-42, 80-2, 88
  equipment 36
  pitfalls 38-40, 88
Prague *31*, *58*, *95*, 99, *100*, 102

Rain *45*, 62, 63, *89*
Reflections in water 20, 54-5, 55
Rivers *6-7*, 12, *12-13*, 14, *21*, *28-9*, *30*, *33*, 38, *51-5*, *60*, 64-6, *64-6*, 67, *71-3*, 80, *81-2*
Royal Institute of Oil Painters 18
Royal Society of Marine Artists 15, 18, 66-7

Sargent, John Singer 20, 93, 95
Sculpture 93, *121*
Seasons 47-8, 80
Second World War 8, *16*, 17
Shadows 42, 54, 58-9, 60-2, 93
Sickert, Walter Richard 36
Sidmouth *51*, 74
Simplification 59-60, 70, 107, 113, 124, 127
Sketches 23
Skies 48-50, 54
  viewing 50
Spring scenes 47, *82*
Still lifes 124-7
Street scenes *9*, *63*, *85*, 93, *101*, *105*, 107
Studio work 26, 80, 123, *125*
Subjects, choosing 42-3
Summer scenes 43, 47-8, *112*

Texture 92
Thames, River *6-7*, 15, *15*, *55*, 64-6, *64-5*, 67, *72-3*, 80
Tides 71
Times of day 46-7, 48, 88, 95, 99
Tones 23, 26, 63
Townscapes *16*, *22*, *32*, 84-105, *85-7*, *89-91*, *94-101*, *107*
  figures in 93, *105*, 106, *107*
Travel 18-19
Trees *1*, 55, 58
Turner, J.M.W. 18, 19, 20, 36, 74, 81, 95, 127

Underwashes 23

Van Gogh, Vincent 14
Vehicles *32*, 93
Venice 18, 19, *21*, *84*, *86*, 93-5, *96-7*, *98*, 99, *99*
Viewpoint 46

Wapping Group of Artists 17, 18, 64-6
Washes 9, 22, 23, 26, 46, 48, 93, 116-19
Water:
  see also Rivers; Seascapes
  movement 54-5
  reflections in 20, 54-5, *55*
Watercolours, handling outdoors 46
Weather:
  conveying 20, 42, 43, 47-8, 80-1, 88
  extremes 102
  perspective in 62-3
  protecting work from 46
Wet-into-wet 50, 58, 118
Winter scenes *10*, 11, *47*, 48
Working methods 23, 26-7
Working position 23
Wright, Alfred 12, 14, 16
Wright, Bert 102

Young, Craig 35